T0049343

DISAPPEARING ACT

A TRUE STORY

DISAPPEARING ACT

A TRUE STORY

JIORDAN CASTLE

FARRAR STRAUS GIROUX
NEW YORK

Farrar Straus Giroux Books for Young Readers
An imprint of Macmillan Publishing Group, LLC
120 Broadway, New York, NY 10271
fiercereads.com

Our books may be purchased in bulk for promotional, educational, or business use. Please contact your local bookseller or the Macmillan Corporate and Premium Sales Department at (800) 221-7945 ext. 5442 or by email at MacmillanSpecialMarkets@macmillan.com.

Library of Congress Cataloging-in-Publication Data is available upon request.

First edition, 2023
Designed by Mallory Grigg
Printed in the United States of America

ISBN 978-0-374-38977-2
1 3 5 7 9 10 8 6 4 2

FOR ME THEN

AND FOR YOU NOW

Remember what it was to be me:
that is always the point.

—**Joan Didion,** *Slouching Towards Bethlehem*

AUTHOR'S NOTE

The first time my father went to prison, I was twelve years old. From the outside, it was a time of collecting comic books, learning to apply eyeliner, and many failed attempts at keeping a diary. I felt like a distant planet, cratered in ways invisible to the naked eye. All around me, life continued. I had friends, crushes, classes I liked and classes I didn't, and a half secret buried inside. The secret didn't feel like mine—I wasn't the one in prison, was I?—but it felt dark and heavy all the same.

I had no survival guide then, no easy answers to questions that felt impossible to say out loud.

For years I searched bookstores for anything that resembled my story. There were prison cookbooks and memoirs written by guards and former prisoners, but nothing for young people like me, connected to prison by a tin can on a string. Only static on the other end.

No matter how you get there or how long you spend there, a personal relationship to prison can carry with it a deep sense of shame and confusion. Time didn't stop, but I froze. I counted hours instead of days. My father didn't die, but he was gone. A black hole bloomed in the center of my life, and there seemed to be no escaping its pull. No one could see it, and I could see little else.

When something falls into a black hole, it's lost.

But the story doesn't have to end there. Given enough time and the right circumstances, a black hole has the potential to evaporate and explode, laying the foundation for a new generation of stars.

I'm writing this because it's the story of me. I'm writing for my mother, who kept me in orbit. I'm writing for my sisters, who didn't choose this life but made it their own. I'm writing for the other children of prisoners who I longed to meet, who I knew were out there somewhere. And I'm writing for you, holding this book, this dying star, this sentence, even as it disappears.

That said, some of the things that happen in this book happened when I was eleven, others when I was eighteen. That's a lot of ground to cover. For this reason, this book begins with a version of me at age thirteen, about to enter high school. I've collapsed timelines and created composite characters in order to tell the most emotionally accurate story possible—while also trying to protect, honor, and acknowledge those who lived this story. That includes my sisters, who were very present in real life. Their personal narratives, their true stories, belong only to them.

I make this book from my memories, to seed new stars.

WHO WE WERE

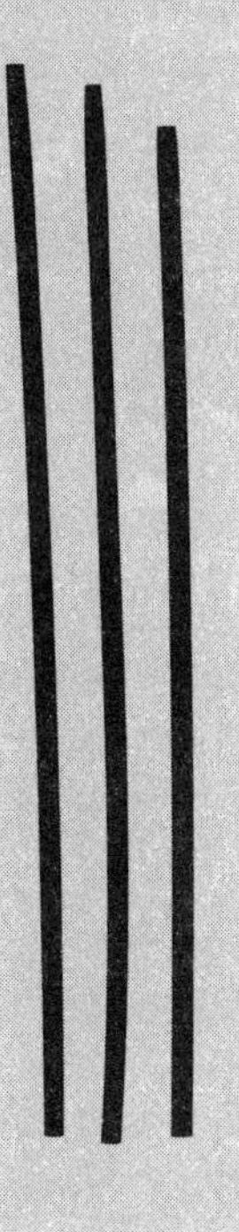

ONE DAY THE DOORBELL RANG

(or did they knock?)

and it was the FBI there to search
for something, or some things.

It was the summer before high school,
the beginning of everything.

But also an end.

They were in the front hall,
then they were everywhere,

their voices booming,

and then it was just

a stampede of shoes
and eyes and teeth on the stairs
down to the basement;

their badges—everything—glinting.

The heavy footfalls
shook my abandoned Barbie mansion

and toppled Power Rangers in line
at the plastic McDonald's drive-thru

as they snaked right
to his office,

only dirt and stems visible
in our backyard flower boxes above—

their hands on his desk,
yanking open each drawer,

their shoes on the floor,
his floor, brought out

the horror movie in me,
the capture the flag in me.

A series of things followed by
a series of things.

    I keep my mind armed
    in case of intruder, and some mornings

    I stick a fork in this memory

and it comes out clean.

I WAS BORN IN THE SUMMERTIME

on a Saturday afternoon
on the North Shore of Long Island.

At 4:11pm
I emerged damp and pink into a white room

with a full head of dark hair.

I went home to a house on a hill.

I had a mom and a dad
and two sisters

and raspberries in the backyard.

This is not a ghost story, though there are ghosts in it.

Years before I was born,
my mom's mother helped her unpack our house.

All I know is that
for hours

a symphony, elaborate—*an orchestra,*
my mom says—

sounded through the house
from nowhere. No radio. No TV.

Beautiful music, she says,
that eventually stopped without warning.

The rest of this story happened too.

MY SISTERS

look like me,
but more like each other.

both older than me,
all of us with brown hair and blue eyes.

Andrea, 20, is all '90s cover girl
in dark clothes and a high metabolism,

energy drinks, and chocolate donuts
for breakfast.

A fast talker with pale skin
she tans; loud like a losing team's coach.

She goes to college for history
45 minutes away,

after moving home from Washington, D.C.

last year when the first college became
too expensive.

Leslie, 17, a senior in high school,

is more earth tones,
more singer-songwriter-poet,

the kind of girl whose guy friends
all have a crush on her.

She's the editor of the school lit magazine,
an artist with pen and paper

and words.
Science says they're my half sisters—
a term some people like to use

to understand quickly,
                too quickly,

to file us   in separate cabinets.

Half
never made sense to me

because growing up we shared
everything—

freckles, rituals, holidays, snacks,
our desktop computer,

a room on a family cruise
when I was seven—

everything.

Except   my last name.
Except   our dad's genes.

MY MOM

I always imagine her taller than she is—
at five foot six they called her the "runt" of her family of giants.

Dark blond hair, sometimes light brown, sometimes
bangs, and her glasses with purple frames.

I have her earlobes. I have her feet.
Matching angles you'd miss with a passing glance.

Not a practicing Jew at age 13,
she missed the traditional milestone.

Instead, she had her Bat Mitzvah
when I was 4 and she was 40.

It meant that much to her.

She was an executive at a bank who took the train
to Manhattan.

I loved the suits she wore,
the shoulder pads like gentle armor,

and this one particular black pendant on a thin
gold chain.

She married two men.
    The second was my dad,

who raised my sisters and me in that house—
like your house, maybe, or not

like where you live
at all, or maybe

like a house you've driven past,
maybe just like that,

with its worn wooden shingles,
its purple flowers,

and the brick path
curling around the hilltop toward the front door.

Full of celebrations and secrets.

WHAT I KNOW ABOUT THE FIRST HUSBAND

He was both of my sisters' dad.
Tall, Texan—he and our mom met
at work.

He was 13 years older than her.
He had a chin just like Leslie's, same V,
same angles. He drank on his boat
and he smoked

and my mom swam pregnant
in their pool. She says she felt light
in the water.

I imagine he loved them all—
my mom and my sisters.

But love wasn't in the room
the time he yanked my mom's necklace
so hard
        it snapped right off her neck.

And then my mom found out
she was pregnant with Leslie,
her *freedom baby*, she says—

a surprise that got her to call her mom,
pack up my sisters,
go home to New York,
and not return.

There was already another man in the picture,
back in the picture—
my dad, who she met in grad school

before moving to Texas,
before meeting the first husband.

They'd been talking on the phone—
about the past,
about a future together.

My sisters still had a dad—

so for a few years they flew to Texas
on summer vacation, days
here and there,

were driven around
and watched and entertained
by the next woman in his life.

This is what I think
I know.
But these aren't my memories.

My dad said he wanted a family,
and my mom came with one
ready-made.

Then came the wedding,
and then came me.

Their first dad faded at the edges
like a photograph:
a phone call on birthdays,

sometimes
a day early or late, an outline
where he used to be.

I think I saw him
when I was really young,

but if I did, years passed
and I never saw him again.

MY DAD

was once a little boy with a black poodle.
I know he had a bicycle too.

Last year he tried to teach me to ride one,
so did my mom—

it didn't stick. Maybe I was too old.
I skipped some of the basics.

Over and over,
I fell to one side in the carless parking lot

of my elementary school that summer,
my helmet hot to the touch,

the color of which I can't remember,
so many hours of ours

I can't remember.

But then some hours I can,
whole evenings,

like the magic show he took me to
when my mom was away for work.

I was seven, maybe eight.

Earlier that day,

he bought me a plush Curious George
at the bookstore in town

where I used to perch
in the wooden fire truck surrounded

by books. The red light, discolored with age
and too much touch,

didn't flash—

    what I mean to conjure now
    is the magic show.

    But I can't see it.

I can't see any of the magician's tricks,
or an assistant onstage, just

the moment he walked out
into the spotlight

and what my dad wore—

a navy blue striped button-down shirt,
the sleeves rolled up.

Soft brown slip-ons: leather with fringe.

And that I held George with both hands
the whole night.

CHANGES

As a family,
we went to temple, we went to dinner,

we went on vacations
with roller coasters and snow tubing and mini golf.

When I was younger
my friends thought my dad was funny,

especially when he got going with a story or a joke,
really theatrical, voices and sound effects,

a balloon high on its own air.

But then when I got older
their faces changed

and he'd go on too long or the joke would get
too strange and they'd nod and smile

and I knew.

My dad wanted us,
but he also wanted more than us.

He had an office in the basement,
where he spent hours writing on legal pads

and shouting on the phone.

The office where we once discovered him
passed out on the floor when I was maybe ten

and I don't know if it was medication for moods,
if it was pills from prescription bottles upstairs

or from the plastic cart down in his office, loaded
with all kinds of pills like a drugstore,

or if it was stress or something else—

    the doctor might have said—

but when he came to,
he didn't know who I was.

He called my mom by her maiden name
and asked me again and again

if he really had children. The illusion lasted all day.

He thought I was charming—
if he ever had kids, he might want one

like me.

HE DIDN'T ASK

when he'd forgotten himself
and me for the day,

if I'd want a dad like him—
what I thought of him

handling other people's money
for a living,

if I knew what he did with it,
if I knew

what his business partners
did with it,

why he traveled where he did
for work,

and once brought home gems
for each of us—

mine was a sapphire chip
in a tiny white box—

another time,
slippers with sports team logos.

None of it made sense to me,
but these were gifts,

not riddles.

FOOL ME ONCE

I can't tell you whether my dad was always a ______. I can tell you that he grew up in a house with a father who was also ______, who heard voices in his head. That my dad thought having money was important, that it made you powerful, like ______ or ______. That it made you free.

My dad went to college and grad school, one right after the other. He played guitar and sang. He taught ______ classes. He got older. There was my mom, my sisters, and me. Like I said, he got into business for himself. With other people.

One of his business partners gave me his family recipe for ______ ______ ______ for a class project in fifth grade. It was the year my teacher said America was a ______ ______, that we each had something special to contribute. Our differences made us ______. My school had kids of all different backgrounds, all different ______. Secondhand ______ seated next to the most expensive ______.

______ business doesn't usually look ______ from the outside. Sometimes there are good intentions that turn into ______ and start to sound like the truth. My dad had ______ intentions that transformed into ______ over the years. Other people had other ideas, ideas that warped my dad's sense of ______. Or he warped theirs.

When that happened, there was more shouting on the phone. He called people names I'd never heard before, even on TV, like ______ and ______. I sat two flights up in my closet with the door shut. Sometimes with a ______ and a book, his voice hammering through the floor below.

If there was silence, I'd tiptoe down to the kitchen and find him with his face in his hands.

After working all day, my mom would get home, eat dinner with us, and type up documents for my dad late into the night. All kinds of documents, some about ______ and some about ______, I guess. He called her real job her ______ *job*, as if it were pretend. Or temporary.

I can't tell you whether my dad was always ______. I can tell you that for years he showed me the reddest and bluest emotions, often on the same day. It felt like falling through one trapdoor and being ______ through another.

There are moments from those years I still can't quite ______, that I recognize only by their ______. I'm trying to hide this story in plain sight. I'm trying to fill in the blanks.

THINGS STARTED TO UNRAVEL

Days after the FBI came the worried looks
between my mom and me,

her telling me we should be prepared
for something, but not how

or even   what   exactly.

Leslie and I each spent more time
with our friends,

fading into the background of
life at our house,

Andrea living her own life
at her apartment a short drive away

in town—above a yarn store,
next to a bar.

All of us trying to avoid the subject,
and so   each other.

I didn't even know what to tell
my friends, like Noelle,

who has a big mouth
but means well.

I don't know what my mom
told my sisters,

if she also told them
something was coming,

like a trailer for a movie
none of us   wanted to see.

After the FBI came my dad's
red face

packing a duffel bag
while no one was home—

I WAS AT MY FRIEND MAYA'S HOUSE

when most of what happened next happened.

Some weeks after the FBI. They felt long and short to me.

Sometimes I think
my mind
remembers to misremember
to remember something safer,
smaller, than the truth.

If you repeat it back, if you write it down, the truth is still a story.

I was on Maya's computer, playing a game where the goal is to blow things up.

The bigger the explosion, the more points.

What I know is this:

My dad left an envelope for my mom on their bed.

Inside: Papers. People to contact. Loose ends to tie up, like a kite string.

And a voicemail, which he said he'd never leave.

My mom once told me she said to him, *If you do this—*
She didn't want to know
because she'd have to stop him.

If you do this.

Sometimes I can forget

that he did.

It was Leslie's idea to try dialing *69—maybe no one else had called. It would only work if he had been the last incoming call. It would automatically redial the last number that had called our house phone, like magic.

When Leslie reached my dad, it was like he was at the bottom of the ocean floor, calling up from somewhere impossible.

A depth I didn't know.

Would never.

He was groggy, he was sorry, he was crying, there were long breaks in his speech, he was at the end of everything.

He was goodbye, he was don't try to save me.

He was at a Holiday Inn not far from home.

I imagine the long cord, the thick black phone in his hand.

His eyes closed.

My mom called me, her voice thick. Then the long minutes waiting with Maya for my mom's car to appear on her block.

Maya waved as the car pulled away, two silver beaded bracelets rolling up and down her wrist.

Maya, three inches taller than me at five foot seven in a black cotton dress with tiny pink flowers on it. Skinny, with big feet and hands. Her dark, fine hair tucked into a low ponytail. Staring back like an Abercrombie catalog model.

She mouthed *Later*
and mimed frantic texting with both hands from her porch.

Her nail polish was chipped, a pink-orange color.

Maya and I met last year in eighth grade when we both made the tennis team. The coach paired us because we were the worst. But everyone who tried out got a spot. School policy.

After our first practice, where I accidentally served the ball smack into the back of her head, she asked me to hang out.

We walked the mile into town and got pizza. I don't even remember what we talked about, just that we laughed a lot. And we were never bored. She dumped handfuls of cold shredded cheese on her slice. So I did the same.

She was the first friend I made I hadn't known forever.
Who didn't already know what my dad was like.

A few months earlier, before the FBI, we adopted a dog.

Maya came over the day we got Peanut, and we spent hours just sitting on the couch together, the three of us.

She left before dinner, before my dad came home and started yelling. About the dog, about the feeling of being watched, about having his phone calls listened to, about dinner. And then he went down to the basement and didn't eat.

My shame, realizing
how badly I wanted it all to be over,
hope and hurt burning a hole in my stomach.

I told myself, *It's okay to let go.* But I didn't believe it.

Some dogs have trouble with overheating and breathing and needing badly to be loved.

Peanut is like that. She came with her name.

She's the color of a roasted peanut with big, dark eyes and a flat face, with a tongue that sticks out to one side permanently. Ever since birth, her old owners said, when we met them at their house and took Peanut home.

She always looks unsure, but her nubby tail moves around, happy, when you pet her.

When they picked him up, he was still alive, full of pills that could've come from the collection in his office, combinations of which he invented.

My favorite were the teal ones, translucent, like jelly beans.

But this time, the police and the doctor said he had taken more pills than I could count.

A panic threaded between all of us, invisible.

Maya texted me a bunch of question marks. I didn't have words. I sent a frowning face. She sent me back a heart.

My chest a conch shell   with no blood   to echo back.

We waited for them to pump his stomach, for him to wake up.

Leslie called her boyfriend, pacing. My mom and I sat on a bench. There was no one I wanted to call, not even Maya. It felt like too much to explain. The sky that night was green gray, like the inside of a puddle.

He woke up angry. The rasp in his voice like a snake's rattle.

I held the plastic straw in his cup of water for him to drink, slowly.

I said, to no one in particular, that *things would be better now*.

Maya had a dog that ran away. He looked like a gray mop, always tangled. I met him a few times before he went missing.

She didn't talk about him much after, but she kept a photo of him on the bookshelf in her room.

I don't know how anyone makes peace with not knowing.

But I guess
maybe it's not peace. Maybe it's something else.

THERE WAS

no envelope left for my sisters or me.

HELL IS THE HOSPITAL VISITING ROOM

and its cheap piano, its dime-store books,
its dime-thin teenage girls,
an old woman
who yelled at her grown son for coming,

and my dad, still drugged,
with the pebbled skin of someone
washed up on land.

The backs of my thighs stuck to a vinyl seat.

In front of the other patients and families,
I saw my mom hold his face
in her hands, eyes closed,
moving her mouth without sound,
praying to a god I'd let go.

I started praying to ghosts
because they seemed more likely to listen,
all air and exorcism.

I'd believed in wilder things,
like palm readers, surviving the weeks left
until the start of freshman year,
a heaven I could touch: Peanut on the couch,

her warm body crushed against mine—
after the cops, after the quiet,
softly snoring
to break the silence.

IN THE PSYCH WARD THE FIVE OF US HAD FAMILY THERAPY

and it was really weird,
like my Studio Art class the year before

except no one gave me an A
or even a B for effort.

We all had to draw pictures that represented
our family,

like orange and red flames,
a green frog. A big black dot.

Andrea refused.
Leslie drew herself just out of frame.

There was screaming down the hall
we weren't supposed to hear.

I can't always remember everything,
even as it's happening.

But how do you feel about what he did?
the woman behind the desk

asked my sisters, asked my mom,
asked me.

Like my dad still wants to die.
And now he's going to prison.

His lawyer said there was a good chance.
Prison. Prison. Like a heartbeat thrumming in my ears.

In movies they say   *don't drop the soap.*
        They say   *sleep with one eye open.*

I can't sleep at night and I'm tired all day.
I'm scared of what I don't know   *and what I might.*

But I didn't say that.

I added more flames to my paper
and handed it over.

And a few days later my dad came home.

WE WATCHED RERUNS OF REBA ON TV

in the living room—my mom, my dad, and me.
Andrea stood on the stairs behind us,
one heavy step at a time,
and spit:

Well isn't this just *the perfect family,*

the words dripping like gasoline,
fire spreading in my chest, the hot shame of it,
like I'd been caught,
like I'd betrayed the rest of us

by trying to be still, a statue in my dad's house,
stupid and stoic
all through the commercial break,
silent as a mistake.

She was right—

I wanted to tell her that. But she was gone,
out the front door, back to her car outside,
back to her life outside, her disdain for him,
it, us, me,

out of my slow reach.

EVEN NOW

I want to tell her that.

MAYBE FIVE YEARS

My attorney says maybe five years,
I heard my dad tell my mom

in their room with the door closed,
the sun going down somewhere

outside, my mom choking, no,
sobbing, then the sound

of her bare feet hitting the ground,
the rest of her slinking down

like an anchor crashing
straight through the floor,

me on the other side
of the door, ready to set the table

for dinner, ready to ask my mom
if I can go to Maya's house

for the night or forever.

MAYA'S FAMILY

She doesn't talk about her dad much, except to say that he's found Jesus since her parents' divorce last year. He gave Maya and her younger sister, Olivia, tiny neon bibles in their stockings at Christmas and joined a men's choir at his new church. She says it doesn't really bother her, because *at least he has something to do other than try to hang out with us all the time.*

Maya's mom works half an hour away, something analytical. Something with databases. Maya says she's so much happier since the divorce—"We all are, seriously," Maya says—but keeps telling Maya and Olivia that it's "*me* time." *Jiordan, it's ridiculous. It's always "me time" now.*

Olivia went through a phase when Maya and I met where she pretended to be a cat all the time. Maya told her *stop being weird in front of my friends* and even though it *was* weird and she was definitely too old to be meowing at us at age nine, it was also kind of . . . awesome? She would climb on the couch, paw at the cushions, and hiss at us while we watched TV.

Are you completely insane? Maya would ask her. But then Maya would start laughing, Olivia would start laughing, and I'd watch them, in love with the whole show.

WE TOOK A QUIZ ONLINE

to see where we should go on vacation.

Maya wanted to end up somewhere tropical
and warm, and I wanted to go into space

where it's quiet and dark.

"That's so depressing," she said,
refreshing the page so we could take it again

and end up in Paris or London.

We sat on the floor
in her lavender room, eating pretzels

out of a bag,
not talking about my parents or

high school starting in a couple of months,

both of us in shorts and tank tops
with the window AC rattling.

"What do you want to do for your birthday?"
Maya asked, tapping *shopping* instead of

museums or *dinner and drinks*
when the quiz asked how we'd spend a Saturday.

"I kind of forgot about it."

She nodded.

“We could go see a movie or—

we could go to Paris,” she said, smiling,
holding her phone up to me.

My birthday always means the summer is ending,
school is starting,

I’m always not ready
for something to change.

I WANTED TO BE

a scientist before I wanted to be anything.
I thought I could cure disease, sickness and sadness, whatever made my dad
reach for the different pills in the drawers in his office,
mix varieties like vitamins.

When his eyes would
gray and glaze like a daydream
or he'd be full of energy, explosive.

An imbalance I didn't understand.

I only knew there were highs and lows, not how high or how low,
or when, or what the trigger might be.

Later, I wanted to be a cartoonist—draw scenes and stories
like Leslie drew for me with colored pencils,
make people laugh. Make my dad laugh.

We didn't laugh anymore
after the FBI,
after the hospital, after he came home,
after *Reba*.

All we did was wait for someone else to decide our fate.

There was a plea deal,
the lawyer said,
my dad said.

Something about *a conspiracy to defraud the United States.*

I heard my parents talking about it in the basement,
the loud whispers through gritted teeth.

Prison. *Should've let me die.*

Selfish. *Our house.*

Bankruptcy. *Divorce.*

Whose fault. *Your fault.*

Your fault.

I did it for all of you.

It didn't matter who said what.

I listened where I always listened, seated at the top of the stairs,
caught between the kitchen floor and the future.

About the plea deal, it sounded like

if you admit guilt,
you can get less time than if you go to trial.

My dad took the deal, which meant

guilty,

which meant a prison sentence,
which meant the sentencing in court—

a judge in a room in a robe with a gavel
adding up charges like a bill.

If you take the deal,

you lose the chance to be found innocent

or take any of it back.

HONEYBEE

JULY 15TH

Last month, all we had to care about was my dad surviving.

What comes next, I don't know—
the sentencing, prison, for how long,
what happens to us as a family.

My parents. Our house on top of the hill.

My mom said they'd probably have to get divorced on paper, like *they'd still be together, but not in a way that would link them financially*.

My sisters and I looked at each other like, *You still want to be married* off *paper?*

Sometimes Andrea drives over from her apartment and we still have dinner together,
all of us except for my dad,
upstairs in bed for hours, asleep or not asleep in the dark,
just a sliver of black under the bedroom door.

Somewhere no one can reach.

And then I text Maya and read before bed. I write short poems in a spiral notebook my mom bought for me at the grocery store. I write about my anger, I write about how lonely I can feel, sometimes about how long it's been since I had a crush, what that was like, sometimes what goes through my mind when I can't sleep. Everything.

I Sharpied a title on the marbled cover last spring when I started writing in it. I called it *The Twist Between*. Between what and what, I don't know. It's my first book.

One day in the future it will go missing from my room
in another state,
in another life,

never to be seen again.

But this summer, I write in it.

My mom always says goodnight before she goes to their room, where I think lately my parents sleep but don't speak.

When I was little and my mom traveled for work, she'd record herself reading chapters of a book for me to fall asleep to. But I'd just stay awake and play the recording over and over, until I finally wore myself out.

Tonight I listen to hear anything and it's just creaky floorboards or a ceiling fan, or maybe Peanut snoring in Leslie's room.

The house is barely alive.

I can hear the idea of Leslie's voice, not what she's saying. She talks to her boyfriend on the phone for hours at night. It seems like their relationship became more serious after our dad's suicide attempt. More hours on the phone together, more time in his car, at his house, anywhere else.

"He wants to be there for me," she told me after it happened, "and it's nice to feel loved for a change." Her voice was thick when she said it, accusatory, though not at me.

I wanted that too.

TWO WORLDS

My mom works long hours
    at her desk

    in her office at a bank,
        one of the biggest banks.

I never thought just how far apart
    the two worlds were—

    the one where she worked,
        and my dad's,

which only existed to me
    on paper,

in the basement, on the phone,
    at midnight, at all hours.

Last spring,

she said it was getting
    harder and harder   to focus on work.

There was a nervous energy,
    like one of them was getting ready

        to snap.

WAITING FOR SOMETHING

I can't sleep through the night, so
I watch whatever old shows or made-for-TV movies are on at 2am

on the small bedroom TV both my sisters resent because neither of them had one when they were 13.

Tonight it's a couple of episodes of *Cheers*, and then when *Cheers* is over,

I almost fall asleep, but I can't.

I tiptoe in my boxer shorts and T-shirt down the hall and then the stairs, creaking only once I reach the bottom.

But around the corner, there's light from the kitchen.

"Dad?" He's seated at the kitchen table, back to me. He motions to a chair.

"Hey, honeybee," he says. "I couldn't sleep." He doesn't ask why I'm up. He has sliced turkey on a hamburger bun, bites taken out.

Every word that floats through my head feels like a lie or a waste. I have to say something, but what?

I want everyone to go away

but I also don't want to be left alone.

He tells me about a medication keeping him up all night and that's why he's tired all day and he *doesn't want to go to prison—shouldn't be sent to prison.* That we all have to write letters to the judge to tell him we want him to stay, that my dad's a good man, don't I know that. *Honeybee.*

Your mother keeps talking about divorce. After everything I've done for us.

He leaves the kitchen first, just a hand on my shoulder and then its absence.

I remember that there's most of a Funfetti cake my mom made on the counter. I also remember the time months ago I cut a piece to eat for breakfast and my dad, already charged like a battery, screamed at me, *If I have fat daughters, I'll kill myself!*

He apologized later, said he didn't mean it,
but the memory had already crystallized
like sugar.

I get sad thinking about that morning, then hungry, and then finally I cut a piece. I eat it with my hands, not a speck of frosting left on the plate.

I don't know what I want my letter to the judge to say,
only what it's supposed to.

DEAR JUDGE

~~*I've known my dad my whole life. My dad always wanted to be a dad. When I was little, he would take me for dinner dates to the Chinese restaurant in town with the pink napkins and*~~

~~*Dear Honorable Judge,*~~

~~*My dad can play anything on the piano. He makes chocolate milk with syrup instead of powder. He keeps the green plastic army men I gave him on display in his office. He tries to help me with*~~

~~*Dear Honorable Judge,*~~

~~*Before he tried to kill himself, my dad would sing all the time in the car.*~~

~~*Dear Honorable Judge,*~~

~~*Love isn't enough. What is? Sometimes I don't want to get out of bed. Sometimes I think it would be better if he hadn't survived. Easier. Or if my mom hadn't let him come home. He's the whole house. I can't tell anyone this. I can't tell you this.*~~

Dear Honorable Judge,

Please

JUJITSU

I can never remember how it's spelled, couldn't remember
even when I was eight and practicing in the dojo
on the mat, my fingers balled into fists,
the sōke telling me to get lower,
to get smaller, to move faster,
to fight my way out.

I earned belt after belt, a stripe of tape at the end, always
a test, then another test, practicing in the den at home
with my nunchucks gripped in one hand, *swing*, then
the other hand, getting better and then worse,
tired, annoyed with my dad—watching and
commentating and wanting to learn too.

Then he started training and we would practice together,
him grabbing my ankles, cuffing my wrists, both of us
whirling around like a top, trying to eclipse the other.
I stood short in my white cotton gi, losing the battle
soon in the dojo between me on the mat and me
in the mirror, watching my palms turn pink.

When I quit jujitsu it had already quit me, the wooden rack
for my belts with my name carved in all caps—the one
my mom bought to display—empty, the belts trashed,
a knotted memory, watching my dad punch the air
in the den, kicking in a circle, a fight
no longer meant for me.

JULY 23RD

My mom's friend from temple comes over
and she pulls me into a bear hug when I answer the door.
My mom hurries down the stairs and says, "Oh my *GOD*" when she sees her and they hug and sway in each other's arms.

She hasn't seen Sarah in months, who we used to see
practically every week at services or a play or a bake sale, always something with the two of them and their other women friends at temple.

More of a phone friend lately, my mom has said.

Phone friends seem more common these days, especially since we stopped going to temple last year. Stopped paying dues, stopping attending events, stopped being members. We didn't have the money to stay.

Sometimes my mom seems pissed about all of it—
the membership, the shift in friendship—
other times, hurt.

Sarah says to her, "Kathy, you know I'd never normally drop by unannounced, but—" and gestures around, a big frown on, "you know, when you need a friend, you need a friend." She smells like licorice in her purple-and-blue tent dress, rainbow bangles clattering together as they head toward the living room.

I sit in the kitchen eating red grapes at the table,
texting with Maya and Noelle about Noelle's weekend in
Montauk with her family.

I hear my mom and Sarah talking low in the living room—

"Is he around?"

My mom says no, well, he's upstairs, one of those days,
and then, "All we've all been put through . . . It's so much
crapola for the girls to deal with."

"And for *you,*" Sarah says.

My mom laughs a sad little laugh. "Right, I know."

"It's bullshit, is what it is," Sarah says.

"You're right," my mom says, indignant, "it's *bullshit.*"

They laugh.

I hear paper crinkling.

"I brought you something," Sarah says. "The idea came to me
after we talked last week."

"Oh it's *beautiful,*" my mom says.

"I know it sounds silly, but you should really try journaling,"
Sarah says.

"Whatever you're feeling. It might help."

After they have coffee and Sarah leaves, my mom shows me the soft leather-bound journal. She says it was good to have someone else in the house. To see a friendly face.

"I don't like journals," I tell her. "It feels like I'm writing a report." The nicer the journal, the more official it feels to me. The greater the pressure. I tell her I only write poems, and I only write them in my grocery store notebook.

"I wondered what you'd been writing," she says.

My dad always says I got the writing gene from him.*

For years, he could fill sheets and sheets of yellow legal pads
with small block letters—
poems, projects, and business plans.

My mom puts her hand on mine, her head on my shoulder. She says, "If ever you want to share any of it with me, I'd love to read it."

*IT'LL BE YEARS

before I understand how great of a writer my mom is,
not just a typist or an editor for my dad.

Years until she emails me pages of her own prose—
and asks me   what I think.

JULY 27TH, WE SEND OUR LETTERS AWAY

Gone—

all of us write one, plus a few friends of my dad's, his sister too.

I ask Leslie if she thinks it'll make a difference at the sentencing next month
and she doesn't know,

but she hopes, like I hope, and we shrug together on her bed. Hope what? I don't want him here, but I don't want him there. I want to be somewhere else, on another planet.

At least we tried, she says.

We race each other in Mario Kart 64, both of us falling off the edge of Rainbow Road,
banana peels and red shells everywhere, booby traps we make and avoid and repeat. She's the better player.

DIFFERENT NAMES FOR PRISON I HEAR ON TV

The Big House.

The Pen.

The Clink.

The Joint.

A threat, a throwaway line

a cop in a movie says to the person
in handcuffs,

fist bruising forehead,
into the back of the car,

and then nothing.

We don't see what happens next,
which doesn't mean

nothing happens.

I prefer my dad's name for it:
Finishing School.

I GOOGLE MY DAD

Because I want to know more about what he did,
if there's a truth out there, because
I never know the truth at home.

Page after page of results and there's nothing new.
I click on the result for the bank's website,
which says *Contact us*

for further information. At the very bottom
of the homepage, there are names listed,
contributors thanked, and I see

my mom's name there. The nights she came home
from work and typed up pages and pages
my dad had written by hand that day.

After dinner, doing homework on the floor
in my room, TV on, volume turned down
on an episode of *Divorce Court,*

I never thought to question her second job:
helping my dad do his.

THE TRUTH IS

My dad told me
before he tried to kill himself

that I was keeping him alive.
He said it a few times,

a thin guarantee—

the words
like a padlock over my lungs.

I sat in the overstuffed chair
down in his office,

many nights after school,
after dinner,

all last winter
and spring, before it happened,

tugging at the buttons
on the back cushion, nodding

as he said, *Everything is shit.*

I'm only alive because of you,
honeybee.

Sometimes his voice changed.
Sometimes he'd say, angrily,

I work so hard and for what?
I can't live like this anymore,

I can't talk to your mother
about this.

I think it would be better
if I weren't around anymore.

Leslie said it happened to her too—
up in her room flipping through

a magazine together, pictures of
the Backstreet Boys brooding

at us, she said or I said,
we both might have said,

I don't know what to do,
but I don't want anything bad

to happen. We all talked around
the word *suicide*

but we knew. My mom knew
when she told me,

I'm worried about your dad.
He keeps talking about it.

It, it. Vague, casual—
always about ending *it*. Like,

why not?

When she was fed up
after the FBI came

and before he went missing,
she said,

We'll make sure you have
a black dress to wear.

She meant to his funeral.

It was the coldest, strangest thing
I'd ever heard her say—

the kind of quick jab,
like a joke,

my dad would say. I knew then
something inside us was broken.

I couldn't stop anyone from anything.

I keep wondering
what or who

would have been enough
to make him want to stay.

AUGUST 5TH

Jiord, my mom says, knocking on my door,
around 9pm. I'm mid-poem,

trying to think of a way to describe the sound
of the air conditioner.

She says, "Can we talk," with no question mark.

She says, "We have to sell the house."

I heard Leslie slam the front door
a few minutes ago, but I didn't know why.

All I heard was my mom:
You think I wanted *this to happen?*

My dad goes out for a drive alone
and my mom comes to me to explain—

we lost a lot of money, my dad lost a lot of
other people's money,

and my mom says simply,
we can't afford to keep our house.

After his sentencing.

Moving sale. Our stuff.

For sale. Our house.

She needs everyone's help—picking what to sell,
old stuff, valuable stuff, our stuff.

And we can start looking at a new house,
but it might be a rental,

we don't know what we can afford,
she says, talking fast,

as if to get it over with, as if she'll break
if I react,

and I think

of the comic books
    under my bed, the Pokémon cards,

Leslie's Nintendo systems in her room,

everything we have
    feeling like a price tag,

like things we once had.

STILL AUGUST 5TH

Mostly, I'm angry.

So angry
that when my dad texts me a list of his fears
at 11pm from downstairs in his office,
that this isn't all his fault,
you know—

I ignore it. I try to sleep with the TV on,
my mom making notes
in the kitchen,
trying to organize a way out.

I hear Leslie come in and go right to her room.

I text her, *This fucking sucks.*
She texts back, *I know.*

I want to scream.

Want to punch a hole in the wall,
like he did once when he was
not himself.

But he wasn't someone else,
I think now.

We stopped saying "crazy" as a rule,
which makes me feel crazy.

Outside, looking in.

A FEW DAYS LATER, THE BLUE-AND-WHITE FOR SALE SIGN APPEARS

at the bottom of the hill, beside the mailbox
and the flagpole, where everyone can see it.
In the living room, the realtor says
our house will sell
no problem,

and my mom says, *That's great,*
and my sisters and I all go stand together
out front, deciding *how messed up* everything is.
I pick at the weeds growing through a crack
in our front step.

The realtor gets to walk around
and think of what to say about our house
to strangers who didn't lose
their baby teeth there, lick cake batter
from a beater, watch cartoons, shave the heads
of Barbie and her friends

or play hours of video games alone,
or go sledding down the hill
in the snow, practically
into traffic, while my sisters yelled,
You have to stop yourself!

My dad went out to run errands—
lately there's always an errand to run, eggs to buy
or a prescription to pick up. His eyes were glossy

when he left, more dazed
than depressed.

It's hotter than the sun, more humid than a sauna.
I can feel the sweat pooling
on the back of my neck, the heft of my ponytail,
the heat flooding my nose and cheeks.

Andrea's green flip-flop squeaks
on the front step as she texts aggressively.
She puts her phone away, leaning her whole body
against our dead willow tree.

"You can stay over whenever," Andrea says
to us, and I nod, and I picture her there—
in her apartment making pasta, burning
tall burgundy candles and tealights
that smell like red wine.

THAT NIGHT

I can't stop thinking what life would be like
if he hadn't been found at the Holiday Inn
and survived—

for my dad
            and for us.

The thoughts make me feel guilty and small,
my chest filling like a water balloon
until I feel like I could drown in it
or burst.

In the backyard,
I text Maya a picture of Peanut with her tongue out,
a regal profile of her flat face glowing in the dark.

I stare out into the skinny trees with bushy leaves
Leslie and I decorated one summer
when I was six or seven

with handwritten notes and paper towels,
a DIY fort that was ruined overnight
in the rain.

That day we listened to "Waterfalls" by TLC
on her boom box on repeat,
singing along,

staying outside for hours,
even as the clouds went dark on us.

I watch the overgrown shrub
in the middle of our yard
where my mom and I found a big turtle

that screamed, actually screamed
when it saw Peanut,
who stood behind me in fear.

This loud hiss,
like a sharp, almost human exhale—
annoyed or maybe

just afraid

we'd invaded the home it worked hard
to find and make its own.

I still wonder how long it took the turtle
to get there or where it came from.

I still don't understand.

How it got there, why it stayed,

and why us.

AUGUST 15TH

Our house sells fast.
My mom says that's a good thing.
Where we live is always in demand:
good school district, easy walk into town,
and whatever else the realtor tells potential buyers.

The family that buys our house is blond,
electrically so. Like *lacrosse and picnics*
and an athletic tampon commercial in LA blond.
Easter-egg-hunt blond. A mother,
two boys, who I see only once through a window.
There's a father I never see.

Leslie and I stay out back with Peanut.
I let the brick steps jut into my back.
I snap twigs and leave the pieces on the dirt mounds
where our long-dead hamsters have decayed
into nothing, I bet. Into more dirt.

The family that buys our house doesn't know this.
Where are their dead pets?

They stomp around in the den behind us,
using outside voices. Like all this is already theirs.

After they leave,
my mom's friend Sarah comes over
and helps her pack up
more of the kitchen and the living room,
while my sisters and I focus on our rooms and stuff
from the basement.

It's the last time Sarah will visit our house,
any house of ours, which is eventually
okay, because as my mom tells me in the future:
Not every friendship is meant to last forever.
Not like Maya and me.

MOST OF THE HOUSES WE SEE ARE DEPRESSING

I text Maya. "But they're in the school district,"
I explain, mostly to myself,
because it's expensive to stay here

but it's where we live. We choose the gray
rental house in front of a nursing home,
a few blocks from my old elementary school.

"You can walk to my house though!!!"
she texts. Which is true—
through the deep woods behind the school.

My dad talks about it like it's an improvement,
even though I know he would hate this house
under other circumstances.

It gets good light, he said,
walking on the carpeted den floor
with his shoes off. *What does he care?* I thought.

He might not have to live here is what
I didn't say to my mom
when we were alone in the new kitchen,

unsticking cabinet doors,
discussing where the coffee maker would go,
and finding old ant traps under the sink.

AUGUST 18TH

"HAPPY BIRTHDAY!"

I wake up in my bed to Leslie launching herself at me,

soft and sudden as a bullet from a Nerf gun.

She's done this on special occasions as long as I can remember—my birthday, Christmas.

"Thanks," I manage, crushed under her spider monkey weight.

Downstairs I can hear my mom in the kitchen. Maybe my dad's down there, or maybe he's sitting on the edge of their bed in his cracked brown slippers,

maybe he's thinking what I'm thinking: that soon he'll be gone,

and I'll keep getting older.

Whatever that means.

I'm spending the day with my friends and the night with my family. It helps to be out of the house, even if it's hot, even if everything's the same when I return.

Noelle and I meet at Maya's house to walk into town to get lunch and go to different stores, look at things we can't buy. The walk is less than a mile, but in summer it feels like forever.

Noelle has olive skin and a black mole on her arm. She hates it, but I think it looks cool, like a chocolate chip. She has dark blond hair as thick as a horse's mane tied in a knot on top of her head. She has wide hips in white jeans and boobs that arrived in middle school, and she's always trying to lose *five pounds, just five pounds.*

"Where do you want to go?" Noelle asks me, tugging at her tank top straps. Her shirt is dark green with light green stars, like they should glow in the dark but they don't. "You want to eat first or walk around? It. Is. So. HOT." She fans herself with both hands.

"Euro?" Maya says, pointing at me. European Republic: the place with wraps and fries we love and a million different dipping sauces, where her mom picks up dinner for us and Olivia sometimes when I'm over. Or she gives Maya twenty bucks and we walk there.

I could eat pizza, but Maya and Noelle like the place with cold cheese more than the place I like with the sesame seed crust and the pepperoni pinwheels, and Noelle isn't eating cheese or bread right now.

Plus, the cold cheese place gives you a hot slice and a whole cup of cold shredded mozzarella to dump on top. Something about the combination is perfect.

"Yeah, that sounds good."

"So," Noelle says, her voice lower, dramatic, "how's . . . everything at home? With your . . ."

Maya rolls her eyes.

"It's okay," I say. Noelle scrunches up her face, sympathetic.

"Actually, I mean, it's not, like, my dad mostly stays in bed and my mom is just—

I guess that part is good because it's weird at home with all of us, but—"

"So, not great," Noelle says. Like she's swallowed a bug.

Maya shakes her head and puts her arm through mine, so we make one twisted pretzel baking in the sun.

"Why didn't you just *get fries*?" Maya says, pulling her greasy paper cone away from Noelle.

"I only wanted a couple," Noelle says, moving pieces of lettuce around in her bowl. "*Sorry, not sorry.*" She doesn't try to take any of mine, either because it's my birthday or because my dad's going to prison. Maybe both.

"Do you guys want to go look at books?" I ask. Maya wants a Frappuccino, but the bookstore has cold blended coffee-milk drinks, so we go.

I usually spend more time looking at the books and they walk the aisles and talk, but we can all hang out for a long time at the bookstore because it just goes and goes—the cafe, the seats upstairs by the shelves and shelves of used books, and the corner where authors come and read. Where I daydream it's me behind the table, me reading to people out loud.

THAT NIGHT

And many morrrrrrrrre!
the birthday song ends,

my mom leading my sisters and even my dad
in the whole sad chorus of *Happy Birthday*

and then *Are you one, are you two,*
are you . . .

before I blow out the tiny spiral candles,
clustered together, fifteen of them—

one to grow on, my mom says.

I want my mom to be happy, happy in her eyes
and not just smiling at me,

and for my dad to fade into the background

of this story,
instead of being ripped clean off the page.

AUGUST 20TH

A week until the sentencing and
all that's changed is I'm a year older.

The judge has our letters, my dad said
his lawyer said.

But who knows what he thinks of them?
If he thinks of them.

I've seen a lot of courtroom dramas,
enough to know when the judge has made up their mind

about the crime and the time
before they cut to commercial break.

UNFORTUNATELY, STILL AUGUST 20TH

It's just my dad, me, and Peanut.

He looks back at me
from the doorway

with a duffel bag full of clothes.

He tells me there are things of his
he wants me to keep

while he's away.

I remember him like this,
sealed moving boxes on the floor,

framing him. *Jiordan's dresser.*
Jiordan's closet.

Over his shoulder, he says,

Your mom already has three children.
She doesn't need another one.

And then he's gone.
I don't try to stop him.

I sit on the floor in my room.
I don't call anyone.

When my mom comes home
from a long day at work,

I tell her he left

but not what he said.

At night, he calls and tells her that he's gone
to his sister's house

to wait for the sentencing.
And when he has to report to prison—

my mind rolls the words over:
report to prison, prison, prison—

he says she'll drive him.

It's not always like the movies,
I guess.

If they don't think you'll flee
the country,

you get to drive yourself
to prison—

which seems like a punishment,
but not compared to being

hauled off in handcuffs.

After he told her and they argued,
she hung up

and sat on the couch, the phone
tipping out of her slack hand,

so I sat there too.

When she cried,
I felt the full weight of her against

my shoulder, and she felt
light,

which surprised me,

because I expected heavy
instead of hollow.

THINGS MY DAD ASKED ME TO HANG ON TO

1.

His Casio keyboard

in its zippered carrying case.
The one with the yellow buttons that bark,
saxophone, and make laser sounds
if you want.

2.

Two beautiful Chinese exercise balls,
the heft
of yin and yang sized to his hands.

I keep them in their wooden box with silk lining.

3.

Another wooden box, this one
with five tiny crystals inside. To hold up
and out toward the sun,

or just to open and shut
and remember.

THINGS NO ONE ASKED ME TO HANG ON TO

1.

When things were calm, or
too calm, like the time

he fell asleep at the wheel
driving us to summer camp.

One *DAD!*

and he jerked awake long enough
to pull over and park.

The medication.

His red car.

2.

His songs, the covers
and the originals.

Guitar. Piano.

3.

My long-gone geckos on his shoulders.

4.

Making jokes to waiters.

My parents, seated together
out at breakfast.

Hot coffee
in white cups with saucers.

5.

Our cedar closet in the basement
with coats.

The burning incense.
The wind chimes.

6.

His blue eyes.
His red eyes.

MY MOM HAS TOLD ME THE STORY

of pulling into the parking lot
of our drugstore years ago

and seeing a handsome man
walking out to his car

and realizing—

That's my husband.

Why they were both at the drugstore,
I don't know, I don't care.

The story is good,

airtight like a jar of doomed fireflies.

I keep that story in one hand
while in the other,

I think of the time a few years ago
we drove upstate as a family.

My dad had become angry, manic,
a 15 on a scale of 1 to 10,

arms wild in the air,
shouting in front of our car—

we were parked in the lot of a glass factory,
where they'd bought me a figurine,
we'd gone on a tour—

my mom in the driver's seat, her knuckles
bright white against the wheel,
my sisters and me yelling in the back seat,

and he was shouting *run me over*

over and over, and by then

even I wanted her
to hit him, I can't imagine she didn't want
to hit him,

but no one hit anyone
and eventually,
we drove five hideous hours home,

us and my perfectly unbroken figurine.

I WISH

we could fast-forward to the part of our story
where this—the hurt, the waiting, the worry—
has already happened and I don't have to guess anymore.

Fast-forward to the part where we're history.

They call it a prison sentence,
I text Maya, *but it feels like a whole fucking book.*

AUGUST 25TH

We get used to my dad being at his sister's.
He texts me goodnight, and long texts about how

he just couldn't *take it anymore* at home
with your mother. But I hear her on the phone

with him, not exactly sweet, but not angry.
It's confusing.

What he says to one of us isn't always what he says
to another.

Maya texts and asks how I'm doing,
and do I want to talk?

It helps to text her, even when it's just about
The Real Housewives of whatever city,

or what classes she's not excited for, which boys
might have gotten cuter, who went where

this summer. It helps take me away
from home in my head.

BECAUSE AT HOME

It feels like we live in a museum
of our former family life.

We are the early years,
the middle ages, fossilized, crystallized

like handprints in wet cement.

The box in the basement
    with Andrea's piles of *National Geographic.*

The Polaroid of Leslie on the fridge,
    her smile, a homemade pizza in her hands.

See that
small hole in the fence

where Peanut once escaped
but then she waited for us to find her

at the front door. Her face light gold in the sun.

The fake hanging plant over the table,
    impossibly green, where I once hid

a clay hummingbird
and never found it again.

A mystery.

Like the bird so badly
wanted to be somewhere else,

it disappeared.

AUGUST 26TH, THE DAY BEFORE THE SENTENCING

I can't tell
how my mom is feeling about all this,

except that we go to Marshalls later that day
to look at spatulas

and candles and bags of decaf coffee
and walk around together

somewhere that isn't the house
where my dad is a memory and

she says she feels guilty and I ask why
even though I feel guilty too

and she says it will be a relief
when we learn the sentence tomorrow,

when the house is calm, when everything
doesn't revolve around him anymore.

For so long
I've thought of my dad as the center

of our home planet—

navigating the rough realities
of his moods and medications—

but this whole time,
    he's been the sun

around which we spin, and spin,
    and try not to get sucked into space.

THAT NIGHT

I repeat the same crimson request over
and over in my mind:

Let us be okay—

until the meaning is lost,
until the meaning is lost,

and only the want remains.

THE SENTENCING, AUGUST 27TH

We meet my dad at the courthouse
with his lawyer. We sit in a small office
looking at each other, my mom with her arm
around his shoulder, as if
he hasn't been living somewhere else,
Leslie between Andrea and me,
all of us
talking about how he looks good, it's
a nice tie, then the lawyer is ready,
we're ready, surrounded by hardcover books
I imagine no one can have ever read
in full,
and I can feel my knees pushing back
against my hands. We stand
and we walk and finally
we're all seated
inside the same well-lit nightmare.

WAITING FOR THE VERDICT

is like being stabbed very slowly
with a dull pencil through a fingernail,

which happened once when I was nine.

The boy who'd done it to me
    silent at his desk while I cried.

All rise might be what the guard says,
I can't tell, I feel lost,

    and then the judge.

    An impossible silence.

And then the swish of his black robes
against the floor.

I flick invisible lint off of my black dress,
which hits at the knee,

look at my mom in her dark blue top,
her tiny gold knot earrings,

Andrea in pocketless black pants
and an ironed shirt.

Leslie in one of my mom's tops
and a dangly necklace,

her knuckles tapping on the bench. We sit
in a row.

My dad sits next to his lawyer
at the front of the courtroom,

so I can only see the edges of their faces,
my dad's clean shave, his dark gray suit.

I watch the judge's mouth open
and swing shut like a wrought iron gate.

It's like he's speaking in tongues.

My dad's lawyer says things like,
husband, father, first-time offender.

Focus,

I tell myself.

Pay attention.

And I do

and I do—

to the glossy wooden pews, which squeak,
to my dad's face, which is boarded up—

to my own fingers, which are
miraculously

still here, tangled in my lap.

I wait for him to say it,

to say it,

to say it:

the months, the few
or the many, what if it's many, what if it's

    more years than high school,

if he gets sick in there,
if he's hurt in there,

    and where is *there,*

if I'll spend weekends
eyes down through faceless security,

where a stranger with a holstered gun will look

    past me

        at the next one, the next one—

I pick my cuticles raw, trace my teeth
with my tongue to make sure

they're still there,

and the judge says something about our letters,
about justice, about victims.

And then he reads the sentence out,
like a family curse.

FOUR YEARS

In the courthouse bathroom, after,

while my mom cries in the hall with her whole body,
tugs my dad's forearm like a lever,

my sisters like stacking dolls I can't hide inside
though I want to,

I feel like I need to throw up, but nothing comes.

The nausea crests like a wave, but it passes.
Being alone in the stall helps.

Hey Jiord, I hear Leslie say from the next stall.
At the sink, we look at ourselves in the mirror.

My chest and neck hot like a gas burner clicked on,
no one home, no one to hear the alarm go off.

Before driving home, we all stop for lunch.
We still have to eat, my mom says.

We don't really talk, except for when the server
asks my dad what he'll have

and he just stares ahead and my mom orders him
a turkey sandwich with Russian dressing

on marble rye—my favorite.

AUGUST 31ST

We won't know where they're sending him, but we know he'll have to report to whatever prison it is after school starts next week.

The lawyer said it could be New York, but also maybe not New York.

New York is big, I said, stupidly.
But no one corrected me.

What type of prison? my mom asked the lawyer after the sentencing.
I didn't get the question at first.

And then she said, *Can't they get him into a psychiatric facility?*
So they'll be sure to help him with his medication.

I'm not going, my dad said, *to a fucking insane asylum.*
It was hard to know what to hope for.

I hear my mom talking about divorce again on the phone with him. She says—

the money owed to the victims, the mounting debt, the lawyer,

you have to understand, but I can tell he doesn't,

he says she's going to abandon him.

She repeats it,

Abandon *him?*

ANSWERS

It's embarrassing how little I know about
what he did, how I only nodded
every time my dad said he was doing *big things.*

That it was *all for us.*

That he was helping people.

I didn't question what that help meant
or who those people were.

When I google my dad's name again, the first result is
an actual castle. A different castle than I get
when I search my name.

This one was destroyed and replaced several times
over centuries. And then something else
was built in its place.

Most of the pictures show beautiful gray-brown,
broken towers. Green everywhere—
the trees, the grounds, all around the perimeter.

I want to stay here in the maze of the castle,
zoom in on the cloudy sky overhead, and then
drop myself at its massive front doors.

But I do what I tell myself I came here to do.

I click away. I keep scrolling.

WHEN I FIND MY DAD

I find news articles about the sentencing
that tell me things I didn't know
I didn't want to know.

They all use the same language, words like
scheme and *concoct* and *investor losses*
and *fraud*. Thousands, no—

millions of dollars.

I remember what my dad said his lawyer said,
what I heard my parents stage whispering about.

I find something about *false documents* and
money-laundering. The other men, his partners,
their names. Names I heard him say at home.

The *conspiracy*, I read, started when I was four.

There are government acronyms I don't know,
and sentences about damage to the environment.
It says my dad was involved in a conspiracy

> *to defraud the United States of taxes*
> *due on hundreds of tons of*
> *chlorofluorocarbon refrigerant gasses,*

or CFCs, they call them. The article says
CFCs are:

highly regulated
because their release into the atmosphere
damages the earth's ozone layer,

which protects people, animals and plants
from the harmful effects
of ultraviolet radiation.

I have to read some paragraphs twice
and even then,

it's like I'm reading through a telescope,
light-years away.

More about my dad's bank,

about *a shell company,*
about *a false loan agreement to conceal*
the receipt of income . . .

Multiple crimes, multiple investors
and partners and victims—
their ages and names, where they're from.

I click on every result that comes up,
collecting the information, the quotes especially,
as if knowing it, storing it,

is enough.

IT WOULD FEEL WRONG TO WRITE ANY OF IT DOWN

I don't.

I keep the words I read in my head.

Defrauded.

    Schemed.

        Conspired.

I don't want to tell anyone what I find
or how it makes me feel—

sadder,
but more curious too.

Closer
and further from my dad.

I linger on
the late nights

he spent in a rage
(or was it   a panic?)

on the phone,
echoing.

When he punched a hole in the wall,
I could see it.

It was a fact.

Now, all these new ideas,
new facts,

new holes in my memory—

or holes I didn't know
were there all along.

ANXIETY

This is what it feels like when my thoughts double
and triple

and my brain starts attacking me

with *what if, what if.*

What if my dad is a criminal?
What if he gets hurt in there?

The thoughts repeat.
They loop until

I feel my head start to burn, my vision gets hazy,
and my breath gets choppy,

a hummingbird I can't catch.

What works is cupping my knees in both hands
and squeezing

and squeezing

and counting 1, 2, 1, 2—

out loud if I'm alone, in my head
if I'm not—

until I feel my bones push back,
forcing me to give up,

to retreat from the trip wire I built inside myself.

DISTRACTION

Leslie is on the phone with her boyfriend, the door cracked.
I hear her talking about how much she misses him, even though
he just drove her home,

she's pissed he couldn't stay longer, and *I'm SO GLAD we have
the same lunch period.*
Fiona Apple sings in the background, her voice breaking.

I don't want to talk about what I found about our dad online.
But I don't want to be alone with my thoughts.

If I asked Leslie to play a game with me, she probably would.
We used to play an N64 game trying to clear the screen of
different-colored bubbles.

The screen would get smaller, the bubbles would appear faster,
and then we'd lose. And then we'd start again.

Instead, I call Maya and we do a magazine quiz—
she reads the questions, I respond, and she scores it.

I get mostly Cs,
which means my love life is in trouble. "I mean, no kidding," I say.

The real trouble is that I like boys and I want them to like me, but
the last time
I really liked one and he liked me, it was seventh grade,

and this girl in our class said I wasn't pretty enough for him, that
her friend liked him,
that I had no chance. Maya and I weren't friends yet

and months later when we were and I told her, she said that girl was a bitch,

but that didn't make the doubts go away. Because that girl's friend got the boy

and I stayed away.

POEM FROM FUTURE ME

Imagine all of this has already happened.
In my time, you're somewhere else.
You're someone else.
I can't change anything.
I mean,
if it happened like this,
then it happened
like this.
I know you're afraid.
I was afraid too.
Honeybee.
That's you.
But that's not me.

SEPTEMBER 2ND

Noelle texts us pictures of herself
in different outfits

for the first day of high school.

"I feel like this one makes me look fat,"
she writes, "*or* it makes me look

like I have boobs???"
Maya texts back a laughing face. She writes,

"You *do* have boobs."
I tell her the blue lace-up shirt with jeans.

"I can't believe it's tomorrow,"
Noelle texts, and a pair of big eyes.

Maya texts me privately: "Are you okay?"
I text back a heart.

We got the news from the lawyer
this morning and I texted Maya that

my dad is going to a psychiatric prison
in Massachusetts, a four-hour drive.

My mom and I were taping up
boxes in the garage, nearing the end

of everything. The phone rang
and I heard her say, *Massachusetts?*

All breathless, rung out.
In a few days, he'll be gone.

She said the lawyer said
medium security

and I said, *What does that mean*
and my mom said, *I don't know, Jiord.*

She looked too tired to cry. *At least*
they'll make sure he gets his meds,

she said. We leaned back
against the wall of boxes.

Family doesn't matter to them.
They send you where they send you.

The lawyer said in different states
there can be maximum,

medium, low, and even prison camps
without fences—

and Andrea asked *why not that*
in a group text to my mom

and she didn't have an answer
because the lawyer didn't either.

Every second ticking faster
        and faster,
                an invisible stopwatch.

Every second, my anger
fades into something gray, something
like loss.

SEPTEMBER 3RD

Finishing school in my head
on the bus ride to my high school.

Leslie gets a ride from a friend
in a full car

and most freshmen take the bus
anyway.

Finish, noun:

an end
        or final part
                or stage

                        of something.

I CAN'T GET MY LOCKER OPEN UNLESS

I hit the door
hard—even if the combination is right.

That's how high school starts,

Maya next to me,
pounding on my locker, laughing,

both of us late for different classes.

I'm in precalc with Noelle
and Maya's in Math A.

I didn't read anything
from the recommended reading list

this summer, like *Lord of the Flies*
or *The Bluest Eye*

and I feel behind all day,
thinking about my mom at work,

thinking about my dad
waiting, waiting at his sister's,

time almost up for us—

so when my math teacher asks me
to solve for *x*

I try to solve for *y* instead
and get the problem all wrong.

In Drawing and Painting,
I sketch a bicycle wheel

in pencil that sucks, even though
the real wheel is in front of me

with its clean lines—
the teacher brought it from home—

but she says, *Great effort,*
and today that's enough for me.

I GET LUCKY THOUGH

Noelle, Maya, and I
have the same lunch period.

Sometimes we sit with other girls
we know, like Catelyn,

who goes to church with Noelle
and Maya.

Except that she's really into it.

She's nice, but she's also
the same girl

who asked me in middle school if I
spoke Jewish,

and why I didn't believe in Jesus.

I don't remember exactly what I said,
except that Jewish isn't a language.

Most of my friends from temple
lived in nearby school districts,

and then
we stopped going to temple.

Even though it's Long Island
and there are a lot of Jewish people,

most of my friends at school aren't.

Religion doesn't come up much,
except for sometimes with Catelyn,

who I wouldn't call my friend.

None of my friends ask me about Jesus
or Hebrew or whether I feel bad

or less Jewish
because I didn't have a Bat Mitzvah

when I turned 13. I had trouble focusing,
couldn't remember basic words

in Hebrew,
let alone a whole portion of the torah,

and my teacher at temple would repeat
the word for "butterfly,"

but I could never catch it.
And when we couldn't afford a party,

I didn't have to struggle anymore.
I quit.

Leslie and Andrea both had their
Bat Mitzvahs as planned—

Andrea with the white fairy-like dress
she hated,

the *Looney Tunes* centerpieces;

Leslie with the little black dress
Andrea was *so mad* she got to wear . . .

Everything covered
in glitter, socks on the dance floor,

and me in my white dresses at both
of their parties, our two parents,

the sheet cake, the DJs,
the money spent when there was

still money to spend.

THE THING ABOUT THE CAFETERIA

is that it's split in two dining sections on either side of the room where you get your food, connected by a long hall. And it seems like one side has mostly Black and Hispanic kids. It's the smaller side. The other side has mostly white kids. Same tables, same chairs, same windows, smaller room. We talk about how weird it is, but we all seem to accept it. I see my friends on the white side, the bigger side. Both sides have murals of flowers and names from former students, lyrics, quotes, all painted on the walls.

In the long hall, I wave at Britt, who I was close with in sixth grade, before middle school, and she waves back. We talk in line with our trays for the hot food in between the two sections and then split off, where she sits on the smaller side with a girl who called her an Oreo in class back then. Said she *acted so white*. Britt has long braids and high-waisted black jeans. The most beautiful smile, like a toothpaste ad.

We used to listen to the radio in her room while we did homework together for different classes. We used to videotape ourselves doing dance routines in the front yard. A boy our age who lived next door had a crush on her and he'd rattle the chain link fences between their houses and call over to us. She always told him to *go away, we're busy*. So sure of herself, just like that.

We never talked about what that girl said, but we don't talk about much anymore. Now it's embarrassing—that I couldn't bridge the gap. That I didn't even see it as it was growing between us. So now we wave and I tell myself it was a misunderstanding, it was time,

when there isn't one simple word for what it was.

SEPTEMBER 5TH

The first couple of days after school
Leslie and I sort more stuff for the moving sale
this month. She plays Counting Crows loudly
in her room so that I can hear it down the hall
in mine. Andrea comes over before work
and makes cutthroat decisions
about what to sell, what to trash, what to take
back to her apartment.
She leaves with several bottles of perfume
and her box set of *Rocky* DVDs.

When we take a break in the kitchen,
eating chips out of the bag, hunched over
the counter, I ask Leslie if she's afraid of Dad
going to prison tomorrow and she asks if I mean
for him or for us and I nod, both,
and she says, *Yeah, Jiord. I am.*
I say, *I'm sorry you got screwed on the dad front,*
oh-for-two and I hope she knows
I'm kidding even though I'm not really, I can't be,
because it's true. *Yeah,* she says, *really.*
I notice her socks have stripes.
She's been taking photos of her feet
lately. She says they're her favorite feature.

She asks me if there are any cute boys in school
this year and I say not that I've noticed,
all the same boys but some are taller,

all the same jock types,
no big whoop. She says, *It could be good practice*
for you to have a boyfriend. And I say,
If I could find *one to like.*
Someone with tight jeans, good music, cool, I add.
Easy, I say. She laughs. *I get it,* she says.
I don't say, *And one who likes me.* I wipe crumbs
off the counter.

MY GOD

Alone in my room on my phone,
I stay up late and read articles about prison
that only make it worse.

How to survive the first day. The first night.

And about my dad's prison:

Federal medical center.

*For male inmates requiring specialized or
long-term medical or mental health care.*

I set the TV sleep timer to 60 minutes,
90,

then turn it off.

Episode after made-for-TV movie
after infomercial plays—

me a hostage tied up in a hallway inside my own heart,
asking no one, *What happens next?*

HOW TO GET TO PRISON

Fastest route now, includes slowdowns and a crash
▸ This route has tolls

- ▸ Get on the street where we saw the deer one time,
  the deer that didn't pause
  like they do in the movies

  before the bloody kill or the elegant escape. It just kept going.
  6 min (2.7 mi)

- ▸ Exit here, where there are only two things: kill or escape.

  Choose neither.
  5 min (5.4 mi)

- ▸ Continue on the highway into a parallel universe, where I'm alone
  in the hall lined with lockers. It's dark and

  a shadow appears. Together we look like poorly
  chosen dance partners—certain only of our own steps. It is

  exhausting. The shadow lunges at me. But I'm ready.
  I've been waiting for this. Wanting it.

  A conclusion.
  21 min (18.7 mi)

- ▸ As if this is a dream.

Follow me into the moment I wake up with my bed sheet draped over my face, fists balled under my pillow.

2 h 27 min (132.2 mi)

▸ In this universe, take the hard right. Exit into the parking lot of the place you'll surrender.

Where, right now, am I?
21 min (13.9 mi)

I FEEL LIKE A MANNEQUIN

in my black sneakers
and gray zip-up hoodie,
my dark blue jeans,
tight at the ankle.
I didn't straighten
my hair.
I put it in a scraggly bun.
I left my eyes
unlined.

Maya props me up
at the entrance to school,
where she gives me half of
a chocolate chip scone
from the good bakery.

"Do you *want* to go in?"
she asks.

We're already late
for first period,
and the security guard
can't see us
but we can see her,
and I say no
but we go because
what can I do?

Where can I be?

We could
take the long walk
to Maya's house but then
we'd have to talk about it
and the words have all
up and left
me.

IN SCIENCE CLASS

I rest my chin
on my desk, face forward,
so it looks like I'm paying attention.

My teacher adjusts his glasses
on his face and talks about erosion.

Destruction that takes a long time. I get it.

But now he's saying
the surface of the earth that dissolves
isn't lost forever—

it's transported somewhere new.

THE FIRST NIGHT

Eating pepperoni and pineapple pizza on triangle plates
with my mom at the end of the day, on the couch,
Peanut splayed out at one end, Leslie at her boyfriend's
for dinner.

My mom doesn't say much, doesn't pretend to be
sunshiney. No *How was your day, sweetie?*
like I'd normally get, because today was, let's face it,
hell. We choose whatever Tom Hanks movie is on
without commercials.

She knows from my aunt that my dad made it,
but we don't know if he's settled or what it would mean
for him to be settled. In prison. I look at my phone
and remember: no more texts, no more calls from
Dad the saved contact.

We don't know when he'll call,
but that's how it works now—he'll call. We'll answer.

A robot masquerading as a human will ask
if we'll accept the charges. We will.

We can never call or call back.

FOR THREE DAYS

we don't hear anything.

Nothing—

not from my dad, not from the prison,
not from the government websites we email and call
to try and understand the silence.

In Drawing and Painting, I add blue watercolors
to my small drawing of a bird,

the wings mismatched but at least in flight.

A boy in my class who touches his mouth with the
wooden end of his paintbrush
every time he brushes the canvas asks
what kind of bird it is
and all I can think to tell him is
not a penguin.

For the first couple of days, I go home after school and Maya
calls me. She distracts me with stories about people in her
photography class.

I want to be alone to lie on my bed and ignore my homework
and people, but Maya isn't people,

and Maya tells me he's probably okay,
it's probably just some rule we don't know, that maybe
he can't call us for some reason,
it's not that he doesn't want to.

SEPTEMBER 9TH

"Are. You. Joking." I say to my mom
when I get home from Maya's
after school, before dinner,
and it turns out my dad was
in solitary confinement,

waiting for a bed to open up.
She's been crying in the kitchen.
Her face swollen,
mascara flecked under her lower lids.
Tissues crumpled on the table.

Peanut at attention below, paws fixed
in place. Neither of us can help.

She's still all dressed up
from work,
like a sad Banana Republic ad
for a gray suit jacket.
Her feet in sheer stockings, propped up
on a chair.

"What does that mean?" I ask.
Something about change of plans
at the prison and *holding*—

that's the word he used
on the phone,
she says—

holding the men,
and there wasn't space at first
and now he's where he's
supposed to be,
hours away from us, alive.

THIS IS HOW I LEARN WHAT TO EXPECT

from the system,
which is
nothing.

A wrench
jammed
in my chest.

I write
in my notebook
all the blues

and reds,
how much I *hate*
everything,

how it feels like
this lump
in my throat

is a new,
permanent part
of my body.

SEPTEMBER 10TH

My mom says the prison has a canteen, or a commissary, like at summer camp, where the men can buy specific goods like clothes and nonperishable food with the money they get from working or that family and friends add to their account.

Now we know where my dad is and what his inmate number is, so she has to figure out how to send money for some of his essentials.

I know she's doing mental math to see what she can afford—how long he'll be able to stretch it.

The government website says she can use MoneyGram, Western Union, or the USPS. Everything costs more than it costs, whether it's extra fees or time or both.

The website also says:

> *NOTICE:*
>
> *It's your responsibility to send the funds to the correct inmate. If the information you provide is incorrect, your transaction might be rejected; or worse, the funds may be deposited into the wrong account and not returned.*

So he can buy a pair of walking shoes, a toothbrush, maybe a roll of Tums, a baseball cap, more underwear; no beans, my dad told her—the only beans are refried, which he doesn't want; white tuna, okay, bagged or canned; no pizza—the only pizza comes in a kit, like an off-brand Lunchable.

The website says it can take *two to four hours* for money to post to his account at the commissary, where *all sales are final and prices are subject to change without notice.*

WHEN THE PHONE RINGS

I answer the phone as if
under a crush of waves

in an ocean
my hands and face

bobbing for air
but

I hear the operator
above and below

her tinkling voice
asking

if I will accept
the charges

seaweed stuffed
in my mouth

ABOUT PRISON—

it's not what I thought it would be, what any of us
thought it would be. My dad especially.

On the phone, he sounds scattered and raspy,
like he needs a sip of water.

He says he gets medication,
but it's not whatever he took before he went away.

He tells me he's scared
and I don't know what to say except that

it'll get better, of course it'll get better,
my lips moving without my brain attached to it,

the words from a script I didn't write.
When I hand the phone to Leslie, there are only

a couple minutes left, just a handful of minutes
at a time. I go to my room

and instead of writing anything down,
I throw my notebook against

the wall.

UNCOORDINATED

Our gym teacher tells us to quit ______ around in the ______ while I'm telling Maya that it's going to be weird to live somewhere my dad's never lived before. We finished packing last night and we have to buy ______ for the new house—new ______, new ______. My mom says we can't afford ______, but we can get ______. The For Sale sign is gone from the bottom of the hill, so it's almost like it isn't ______. But it is.

My legs are bright white in the sun, like a ______. Maybe it'll be good to move, she says. I say, I don't know. I've never lived anywhere else. I want my mom to be ______. I don't want us to be ______. I get it, she says, but she doesn't, she can't, because her parents are divorced so it's like she has two houses and I'm losing the only one I have.

Then ______, the tallest boy in class, kicks the ball straight across the field at us, fast, where it hits me in the ______. The gym teacher shakes her head at me, blows a whistle, and it's as ______ as it was in middle school, when I was also bad at ______. I figure this is going to be a ______ for the rest of the year. But Maya gets to walk me to the nurse, where I ice it until I don't feel anything at all.

WHEN I'M GOOD AND NUMB

I walk to English class, late,
where it's quiet—

a free write.

My teacher points to the board,
where it says,

Write about a place you love and why.

This one is easy.

I write about Maya's room,
specifically the floor,

where we eat snacks she assembles
from random ingredients in the kitchen,

watch bad movies, try out makeup,
take quizzes,

talk about who we're going
to be, what we'll be famous for.

I write about last winter,
when I read her copy of *Speak,*

the whole thing,
while she watched TV and took photos

on her old digital camera.

Right then,
that day was my favorite place to be.

My mom and dad weren't fighting,
they couldn't fight—

my dad was on a downswing,
lights off, in bed,

and I didn't want to be home.

I spent the whole day at Maya's,
and she only interrupted me

to ask what I wanted to eat
for lunch.

HOW WAS YOUR DAY?

I hear my mom's tone on the phone
after dinner. Short, low.

"I can't *do this right now,*" she says.
"Well, it's *never* a good time,

is it?"

When she hands it over to me,
he says he loves me—

I love you,
I love you.

Each word sticks like a dart in a board.
I think about what I did all day,

different classrooms and faces
and going to Maya's after school

to watch TV, and how he's been
stuck in one place.

Every time I have this thought,
I feel guilty.

We're almost out of minutes
before we even start.

I tell him about school—
about drawing contour lines

and not about gym—and he asks if I'm
reading anything good.

Not Shakespeare for class,
which I can't make myself care about,

even if the story is interesting
on the surface

(the couple dies at the end—
    I read the summary online).

I know enough to talk about it,
fake opinions, speak up from the back row.

But what I care about
is the book I'm reading just for me.

It's called *The House of the Scorpion.*

I tell him it's for kids and teenagers,
but he wants to read it too.

Would I send him chapters as I read them?

JUST ONE OR TWO CHAPTERS AT A TIME

he asks,

so he has something to look forward to.
　　So we can talk about it when he calls.

After I hang up, my mom brightens.
She says, "That's a great idea."

I imagine each chapter, ten to twelve pages,
will take several days to reach him.

The mail, 　　　the *inspection* of the mail,
and then to my dad in his cell.

I can't use staples.

Staples aren't allowed—no sharp metals
or even bits of string.

From the rules my dad reads and repeats,
it sounds like almost anything can be used

to hurt someone.

"What were you talking about before?"
I ask her. "With Dad."

"Oh," she says, "he just doesn't get it."

"Doesn't get *what?*" I say.

"That I'm tired, that I need a break," she says,
exasperated. "But it's all so hard on *him*.

It's never as hard   on anyone else."

THE HOUSE OF THE SCORPION

Matt, the main character, wasn't born like other kids—
he was harvested.

His DNA came from an evil ruler. He's a clone.

He spends the first few chapters trying to make sense of his life,
but under constant threat, afraid of the evil ruler's power-hungry
family.

We learn early on that escape is the only chance he has to
survive.

And though you want him to escape—because he's likable,
because he's the hero of the story—

escape doesn't guarantee him freedom.

There's an invisible question threaded through every page
about who Matt wants to be,

and whether he even gets to choose.

HOW IT'S DONE

I rip a few pages out of the spine
at a time,

watch them hollow the book little
by little, until I have the few chapters I've read.

I'm doing the right thing.

But I hate ruining a book,
especially one my mom gave me.

I dog-ear the stack to keep the pages together.
I slide them into a business-size envelope,
the pages folded flat, like an oversize deck of cards.

My dad and I might have this,

but I can't see anything keeping my parents
together.

FOR THE MOVING SALE

It's not time yet, but the hall is packed with stuff
to sell. My mom collects all the books, CDs, toys,
and shirts my sisters and I have piled in trash bags
and boxes and moves them into the garage.
Together, we come up with prices
and she writes them on stickers. *Be reasonable,*
she says. We haggle with ourselves,
Leslie and me trying to
drive up prices—look at this, it's mine, it's *worth*
something, we argue—and my mom brings us
back to reality, says it's worth
what someone will pay. Ten dollars for a lamp,
twenty dollars for the complete series of *Friends*
on DVD. My mom is like a surgeon, ruthless,
selecting the right tool, shaking us free
from the memory of an old sandwich press
that melted turkey sandwiches into seashell shapes,
or a pair of bejeweled high heels from a party.

But it still feels like preparing to sell off pieces of us—
who we've been in this house, in this family,
to our friends, to myself. My *Archie* comics,
my binder full of Pokémon cards,
most of the CDs I had
in the soft red zip-up case from Leslie's Bat Mitzvah.
The theme was *around the world,* with centerpieces
for different cities.
The Eiffel Tower, the Statue of Liberty,

stuff like that. Big, beautiful foam pieces that glittered
on the video years later,
the day we danced to Billy Joel in bare feet and socks,
my chunky kid heels cast off and left at the table.

IT TURNS OUT

I'm not good at math anymore. Science and history
are easier to fake. I can write stories about things,
explain away dates and formulas with enthusiastic
sentences. But math is embarrassing.
Embarrassing when the teacher asks me
for the answer and I don't even understand half of
the problem, Noelle has to kick my foot,
whisper, *It's the radius.* It doesn't help. I say sorry, I say
pass, I shrink into nothing in my seat. *The radius?*
I mouth to Noelle, but the class has already
moved on.

SEPTEMBER 15TH

I wake up feeling like my whole body is made of lead. My head feels thick and heavy, like the flu without a fever. Just a haze. My mom tells me to stay home.

My dad gets the pages in the mail and he calls in the middle of the day, when no one would normally be around. He says because the lines can get long for the phone, sometimes he takes the chance to call when there's no wait. Just in case.

His voice is low and gruff. He says he has a bad cold. He says he's glad it's me. "Honeybee," he says, "I miss the sound of your voice." He sounds relieved and sad.

Thanks, I say, too clammy and tired for his intensity. I feel like I could fall asleep right here in the kitchen. Like I could split in two and one of us could talk and the other could rest.

It's hard to know what to say to someone whose life is like a snow globe, completely still unless shaken. The thoughts repeat in my head, faster, insistent:

Everywhere I go is somewhere he can't go.

The food I eat. What I watch.

Everywhere he goes is a place I imagine in my nightmares.

Even the library, which he describes as the land that time forgot.

Old, dusty, and messy.

I tap my knuckles on the kitchen table. Peanut trots in and trots back out, barely a pause, no food to be found and begged for. I want to go with her.

He tells me what the weather's like there, that his lunch was potato based, and that he's just finished the second chapter of the book.

The book is what I know how to talk about, it seems.

It exists in both worlds.

"I like Matt," he says, coughing. "Will I keep liking him?"

I'm four chapters ahead, but I just say, "Yeah, I do." I chew my cuticle. "He's the hero." I chew too hard. I look at my finger, the skin pulled taut and torn. It starts to bleed.

Stupidly, I ask, "How's it going there?" and hold my breath in my mouth.

He talks about threats I can only imagine, like skin rashes and angry guards. When he says this, I picture bad guys in movies, like dirty cops and home invaders. A block head with a vein bulging from the forehead. No real face I can conjure. Someone cowering below.

Aside from that, there's not much to tell, he says, just that he started playing music with a group of men who think he's good on the guitar. They have instruments in a rec room there, where sometimes he's allowed free time. "Not too many missing strings," he says, "and a lot of talented guys."

He asks how my mom is, even though they spoke last night. I say fine, I guess. I feel strangely protective, thinking about my mom busy at work.

He says, "She's losing patience with me."
I don't know what to say.

We hang up, his snow globe tipping over in my mind, blurry as a wet windshield and silent.

SEPTEMBER 16TH

After school, Maya and I walk the mile
into town and get pizza: mine a ravioli slice,
hers chicken and tomato,
and sodas in tall waxy paper cups.

I tell her I'm failing precalc.
"I've never failed *anything*," I hear myself whine,
cheese catching on my chin.

After another quiz with only a few right answers
I guessed at—red Xs and question marks
all over the page, front and back—

my teacher said I might do better in an easier class.

"Ooh! You can be in my math class,"
Maya says, gesturing to herself
with the wrapper from her straw.

"And then you'll do *really well*," she says,
picking at her nail polish, "especially compared to,
you know . . . like, Ryan."

Ryan, this loudmouth in gym shorts
who's made fun of me for years,
every chance he gets,

for falling asleep on the bus
when we were little.

Like I give a shit. Except that I do.

And he waits for an audience to bring it up.
Winds up like a stupid toy car
headed straight for me in the hall:

"That was *so weird,*" he'll say,

looking for anyone to join in and laugh
at his found memory,
the one I buried. Not deep enough.

I had a hard time sleeping.
I'd go to school tired.
I'd come home tired. I still do.

"Math *A*?" I say, face crinkled, not thinking.

"What's wrong with Math A?" Maya says.
"It's not *precalc,* but who needs precalc."
She's got me there.

We sit for a while,
talk about the weekend, maybe going to the movies
and then hot chocolate and curly fries at the diner—
the one with a personal jukebox on each table.

I check my phone. Still early.

"Let's go look at books?"

"Okay," she says, taking both plates to the trash,
the orange oil stains disappearing
like a sunset.

MAYA AND I SPLIT UP

in that good, unspoken way we do in bookstores
and clothing stores,

and then return to show each other
strange or funny or surprisingly great things.

Between Psychology and Sexuality,
I find a thick paperback about trauma, how it lives

in your body.

The font is tiny as I flip through, catching words like
isolation and *abandonment*.

I'm reading a section about breathing
 when I hear someone say, "That's a good one."

I notice his wrists first,
and the black watch with a big face

on the right one, a beauty mark there. He has tan skin
and shaggy, short dark hair pushed back.

Glasses with thin metal frames. A black T-shirt
with a band name I recognize and

dark, tight blue jeans I can tell
are expensive.

He looks like an ad for the kind of boy I like
but never see at school.

"You've read this?" I ask.
I'm very aware of my beat-up sneakers.

He tilts his head to look at the cover.
"Ahhh," he says.

"I'm thinking of a *different* trauma book
I read for school."

I smile. "Right."

It turns out he's not kidding. His name is Chris
and he goes to a private Catholic high school

for boys. He's a junior.
He's taking psychology as an elective.

Something about him is familiar,
like a song I forget I know

until I hear it on the radio.

WE TALK ABOUT MUSIC AND MOVIES AND

it doesn't feel like any of the other times I've liked someone. I like his *brain* and the way he moves. Talking to Chris feels natural *and* nerve-racking.

He stares right into my eyes, like I'm talking through them
about bands I like, that he likes too, and movies with really good car chases.

When I ask if he's super religious, because of his school,
he says no, but that—"funny story," he says:

his mom was going to become a nun before she met his dad,
and I think that's *so interesting*.

It turns out he lives near my house, *my soon-to-be old house,* I think,
and I know exactly where he means. He has money, he must,

and when he asks where I live, I say I don't know, and he laughs and says
what do you mean, and I say it's a long story,

and he asks if I'll tell him Friday night. I float up out of my body
as I read off my phone number like an alarm code and watch him type it

purposely into his phone. I look down at my sneakers, the white rubber dirty,
the black canvas worn. Distressed.

He texts me on the spot. "So you'll have it," he says. *Hi!* it says. *It's me.*
Like *me* is someone I already know.

I see Maya a few display tables behind Chris, in the humor section, slow waving at me, pointing at him with a *Who's that?* look on her face.

He says he'll text me about Friday, and I nod like a plastic dog on a dashboard, try to make my smile appear casual.

When he's out of sight, Maya appears, her eyes wide.
"What was that?" she says.

We walk to the back corner of the store—where the children's section is, where we're too old to sit in the fire truck, even ironically.

I flip through picture books without looking at the pages, newly wired. Like my chest is on fire.

"Friday?" she says. "I thought we were gonna hang out."

I start to say sorry, could we hang out on Saturday after the moving sale, but she waves me off. "No, no, I get it."

I tell her we have so much in common and where he lives, where he goes to school, that he seems cool

but also nice?

"But it's not a big deal," I say, afraid I'm getting ahead of myself.
"Maybe it's not even a date. Maybe he wants to be friends."

Panic creeps in, slowly at first—and then it fills my whole stupid body.

Maybe he wants to be friends.

"No," she says, rolling her eyes. "He looked emo.
He asked you *out*. He likes you."

I find myself more into boys whose clothes I could wear,
whose style isn't . . . I don't know, macho?
That's not really Maya's thing, but she gets it. She smiles,

flicking her hair behind her shoulder. "I know. You love guys like that."

WE WATCH *JEOPARDY!*

Andrea comes over for dinner and the four of us sit on the couch eating ______ with Peanut snoring on my mom's lap. I don't know the answer to any of the questions, except for this one: ______ ______ in ______. He plays a man who doesn't know he's on a ______ ______. His friends, family, even his coworkers, the neighbors' ______—they're all in on it.

My mom and I saw it ______ times in theaters together, just the two of us, her hand on my arm, my hand in a box of ______ during the scene where the boat crashes right into the ______. Like the end of ______ and the beginning of ______.

I don't know how you keep going when your life becomes something you don't recognize.

I guess he doesn't though. He talks to the ______ of the world, who tells him about the ______ where he lost his first tooth. I push my tongue against my baby tooth, the one my mom let me keep when the orthodontist said it had to go for ______ and ______. She told me that the same thing had happened to her when she was a kid, but her mother made her have the surgery. Except her mother called it a "______," so it would seem less scary, but no details.

How my mom must have felt waking up in the dentist's chair—the "______" a success. Just a kid wearing ______, a bloody mouth, not sure what happened.

My mom always gives me the details. The big picture and all its colors.

She gets the answer to some of the questions right. Andrea shouts them out before the contestants have a chance and she's mostly ______. *Andrea!* my mom says, laughing. If she had a buzzer, she'd be the ______. Leslie and I don't ______.

After dinner, Andrea helps my mom put together folding tables in the garage for the moving sale. I hang out with Leslie in her room. I tell her I met a boy at the bookstore and she says he sounds ______. She doesn't seem worried about whether he's a ______ or a ______, just says she's excited I'm excited. Like maybe he's just a good person. Leslie's boyfriend is a ______ player and they have the same friends at school, for the most part. They look good together. He's ______ to her. I've never met anyone like Chris. *Maybe he'll be your boyfriend,* she says. I tell her he's almost her age. She says, ______.

Boyfriend, the word like a ______ in my head.

I TELL MY MOM

and when I say he's a junior at another school, she doesn't flinch.
I tell her how he dresses, how he seems smart,
what school he goes to, where he lives. How he asked
for my number and it was cool but not *too cool.*

He wears a *watch,* I say.

It's nice to see you excited like this, she says.
I wonder when she was last
excited like this.

THE NEXT FEW DAYS ARE A BLUR

I switch into Math A with Maya,
where I swear the air in the room isn't as thick.
I can breathe here.

The problems on the whiteboard look like things
I remember, could even work out on my own
without having to copy off Noelle's homework.

My sometimes-bully Ryan is here, in theory.
Maya says he skips class a lot
and sometimes he's really obvious about it.

I only see him for a second today
when he yells, "Maya! Maya!" from the doorway
because she's the last to class

and throws his take-home test in her direction.
As if she's going to hand in his homework
so he can go wherever he goes when he's not here.

It lands on the floor and then he's gone,
his shoes smacking all the way down the hall
and out an emergency exit

and our teacher turns from the whiteboard to ask,
Was that Ryan?

Someone says yes and our teacher asks,

Well,

    is he coming back?

and Maya says *NOPE.* We dissolve into laughter.

MORE PAGES

Late, when I'm writing in my journal,
my mom knocks on my open door. She sits on my bed
and asks about Math A and how it's going.

She asks if I've sent more pages to my dad.

I tell her I'm a math genius now and that I've read more but I haven't sent more.

She says, "Jiord, you should really . . ." and I sit up on my bed.

I should really *what*.

"Never *mind*," she says with a sigh.

"No, *what*," I say. "I'm finally doing okay in math and I'm writing and now you want me to feel bad about the book?"

"I didn't say that."

"You tell me about *him* and he asks me about *you*," I say. "Can I not deal with this for *one night*?"

She looks upset. I went too far.

I'm sorry, I say.   No, no, she says, I'm sorry.

She says she's going to go write in her journal and says goodnight, she loves me.

I say it back.
We always say it back.

I notice most of my friends don't say it to their parents when they hang up or when they leave the house. I never realized until recently, until my dad left, that we say it to each other all the time.

Love, love, love, like a wish.

I text Chris questions about his favorite pizza place in town and he asks if I've seen this one foreign movie and it turns out we both like making mix CDs for people.

I don't tell Chris about my dad, just that my mom and I are moving.

I tell him where, sure he'll think it's a downgrade, and all he says is, "I hope I can come see it when you move in."

And I smile at my phone, as if it can see.

I go to bed after midnight and I have strange dreams about prison, clipped like movie trailers—faucets and grass and locks, everything tinged with gray like a highway.

SEPTEMBER 20TH

My mom sounds *at attention*
when she talks to my dad tonight,
like he's a traffic cop
or a bill collector,
no laughter on her side of the call.
She gives the phone to Leslie
quickly and retreats
to her room and shuts the door.
Leslie takes the most minutes
this time, and when she passes
the phone to me,
she squeezes my shoulder,
and in the minute we have left
my dad asks, *Do you miss me?*
Do you still love me? I say,
Yes, of course I do. Dad, of course
I do. Like a doll
pulling its own string. He says,
I don't think your mom does
anymore. Tomorrow is Friday.
Chris. Friday. Friday.
I feel my throat tighten, to keep me
from crying. I hear the warning
our time is running out
and we say goodbye and hang up
and I text Chris because
Chris doesn't know

about my dad and I want
to live in *that* reality,
where I'm just some girl
with a trauma book who maybe
nothing traumatic has happened to
yet.

HIS TEXTS

are full
of questions—
about favorites

and firsts
and family
and friends.

Full sentences,
commas, and
emojis

I can see—
no guessing game,
no hypotheticals,

just the words
exactly
as they are.

I feel desperate
for it,
like writing

in a diary
that thinks
and talks back.

FRIDAY

His text said dinner and a movie. I've never had dinner and a movie
with a boy. Maya texts, *What is he, 40?* And I say, *I think it's nice.*
She's had dinner and a movie. *Yeah, but that was different.*

In middle school, with other people. A group thing.

I call her after school, not to talk me through what I should wear
but what to do if he wants to kiss me, how will I know it's for sure
a *date* and not some kind of misread friendship thing.

There's an edge in her voice when she says, "I have to go—
my mom's taking me to Cate's in a sec." *Cate?* I ask.

"Yeah, Catelyn. Just a few of us hanging out," she says.
"You were busy. So."

I don't know why I'm jealous, especially when I'm going out
on this thing that might be a date. Which is a big deal.

If it's a date.

But it's Catelyn. Catelyn who buttons shirts all the way up to the collar,
who means well. Whose house has an actual white picket fence.

I wear a black tank top with dark jeans. I pull my hair to one side,
like a curtain over my shoulder, thick, unmanageable
but other people say they like it.

I slide on a thin gold ring gifted to me by my grandparents,
a showy I ❤ U etched in the band.
Something shameless in its declaration, to talk of love as if it is

and not as something that was.

I ORDER CHICKEN FINGERS AND THEY GIVE ME A WHOLE PLATTER

so I have a serving tray of eight huge chicken fingers spread out like I'm personally sitting shiva at the restaurant, enough food in front of me to feed a whole host of mourners, and the restaurant is more like a pub, and Chris gets a club sandwich with a salad instead of fries.

He asks me why we're moving, and I think of vague reasons I could give, what I might tell a stranger, like

didn't need the space or *to try something new*

but those seem impossibly adult and impossibly fake and empty and I hear myself say, "My dad went to prison and we can't keep our house" like breaking a dam and watching the water rush out—

or in, depending which side you're on.

"Shit," he says. "That's a lot to deal with." He cups his chin in his hand. Like he's thinking it over. The silence is nice, actually.

He wears a black button-down and dark blue jeans, a leather band on his right wrist. His hair is full and wavy. I want to lace my fingers through both sides. When he speaks, I find myself staring.

His laugh is short and choppy, like its own little joke, one I want to be part of.

He has two older siblings too. We talk about what it's like to be the youngest of three. I don't know what it means to be a family, I tell him. That I think I'm bad at it. That I couldn't save my dad or steer us away from the wreck, that I get why my sisters are so angry with my mom and why I'm so angry with my mom but that I also feel for her, that I have to keep that love in front of my eyes or I'll explode, like when she closes the door to her room at night,

I imagine her years from now, in a different house, in a different life, and I'm there too—the daydream so specific I give myself bangs and they're perfect—and I remember that she's a daughter too.

That she was once so in love with my dad she took her two little kids and moved them to a new life. That she chose him every day for years. Him.

Which meant not choosing us. Or if I'm feeling generous, trying to choose us all but failing. "Does that make sense?" I ask Chris.

He nods. He says, "I bet I would feel the same way," which makes me happy.

I think, sometimes, we all resent her for that.

We show it differently. Andrea yells and says *always* and *never* and Leslie cries and asks questions like *How could you?* and I go silent or I say the wrong thing. Like a benchwarmer in a team sport. I understand the rules of the game, but it doesn't mean I get any better at playing.

Chris nods slowly, like he understands. He says that's romantic, about my parents, and also, really sad about the rest. My sisters. Me.

He asks for the check so we won't be late for the movie and takes it from the server in

one fluid motion,

so cool but also genuine, moves I didn't know until now.

"You're good at"—I gesture between us—"this."
He looks confused.

"Dinner. The check. Feels very adult." I feel stupid for having said it, even though it's true.

He tells me he gets it from his dad. His dad who, he says, is very smooth. "I try to be like that," he says.

My dad has been smooth. Other things too. I can't imagine Chris punching a hole through a wall. I can't imagine him wanting to.

We walk the few blocks to the theater, and he takes my right hand in his left, our fingers clumsy in each other's grip,
but I guess it's a date.

Once I have the thought, I'm afraid it will go wrong. I hate this about myself. Anxiety. That I'll say too much or he'll lose interest. How I'm afraid those aren't even the only two options. He could turn into someone terrible. Or he'll tell future girls about me. About my family. Or I won't even make the footnotes.

But on the escalator up into the darkness of the theater, I focus on his thumb over mine, the feeling already fuzzy, like a memory.

"BUT DID HE HAVE TO KILL ALL OF THOSE PEOPLE?"

I tell Chris *Are you serious*, yes, absolutely he did. He had to kill everyone to get to his daughter. There were no choices, only actions. Only consequences. What kind of person, I ask him, wouldn't kill everyone to save someone they love? He shrugs as we exit the theater.

When we get to the corner, he starts to bend down like he has to tie his shoe, but they're slip-ons, and instead he presses his mouth against mine. A slow pressure building behind my lips.

It feels like the first time I ever watched a magician on TV separate a woman's body. Wonder and terror warming my whole chest.

A cross between *Is she okay?* and the bright flicker of *Don't tell me how it's done.*

AT THE MOVING SALE

in the morning,
Maya stops by and I break
from the table
to tell her more about
the date
than my text of
!!!
could explain last night.
He wants to hang out
again, I say. *I think*
it's a THING.
She says, *That's* so *great,*
stressing the *so*
and asking if
I want to come over later.
A little boy
buys all my Pokémon cards
for twenty bucks
with his mom
and I watch them
disappear down the hill
with the thick white binder
in his arms,
the cards inside
sorted by element
and then by health,
the weak ones
toward the back,

some first-edition
holographics
I should've taken out
and saved,
the cover art
I collaged myself
years ago
with Charizards, Bulbasaurs,
Jigglypuffs,
and Eevees I carefully
cut from issues of
Nintendo Power.
I think about the kiss,
the movie,
who I would kill
to take back
the holographic Mew
in the pocket
inside the binder,
protected by plastic,
Just the one, I tell my mom,
that's all I wanted,
and she says, *Let it go*,
as if I have
any other choice.

YEARS FROM NOW

My mom will tell me it was selling our American Girl
doll stuff that broke her heart. Mine was Felicity,
Leslie's was Samantha. Felicity rode horses
and Samantha was rich. Victorian?
These dolls with their stories, their books,
their accessories. Hairbrushes, suitcases, a horse
with a saddle and stirrups.
Leslie will have wanted them for her kids,
just in case, and I'll have wanted my Pokémon cards
if only to look at them, protected in plastic.

WEEKEND

I tape up the last few open boxes I have
containing my little green stuffed hippo
and so many stuffed zebras,
an old music box from Disney World,
my dad's keyboard, half-empty notebooks,
a couple of tubes of lip gloss—
anything not nailed down or in drawers.
Everything except
my everyday notebook,
where I write about the kiss, Chris,
and losing my only Mew card to a stranger.

Peanut watches from the floor,
edging toward the boxes and then
running away as I tear off bits
of packing tape. I text Chris and Maya
different updates
about the progress, promising to hang out
with each of them this week
after school.

We don't hear from my dad
all weekend,
which makes me feel the horrible mix
of fear—the *what if*
that loops through my dreams at night—
and relief. The silence a threat
and a gift.

My mom says, *I'm sure he's fine*
but crushes her napkin in her hands
at dinner on the couch,
a depressed mountain range. Leslie says,
How do you KNOW. My mom says,
I DON'T. Leslie says, *All we do is worry*
about him, what about us, a question
with no answer.

Leslie gets a text
and says she's going out
with her friends. My mom says, *Good,*
have a good time. Drive safe.
She doesn't ask when she'll be home.
It feels like we have an unspoken rule:
just come home. That's it.
More of a promise than a rule, really.
At least that's how I feel.

I finally tell my mom, *Maybe it's just busy,*
you know how it is, with the phones, I mean.
We lie to each other
and watch *Galaxy Quest* because it's on TV
and because we both love the team
hurtling back to Earth,
rewinding time,
barely saving themselves from collapse.

POEM FROM FUTURE ME

You'll be a writer.

You already are.

You'll get kissed more.

Wear yellow. Wear it now.

Even if you think you look bad.

You love yellow.

What else?

Money matters

because security matters.

Enough is enough.

One day,

you won't have to answer the phone when it rings.

I know what you want.

I can't tell you what happens to Dad,

just that

you'll survive.

SEPTEMBER 24TH

Because we haven't heard from him since last week, I write. I write letters sometimes. Letters are separate from the book. Letters can be short. Letters are a way of talking without having to speak. I get to think and eliminate things and then seal it up and away. Gone.

I don't write about the moving sale, about the Pokémon cards, or how I let it all slip out of reach. How all my comic books sold too, except for the single plastic-wrapped *Archie* issue I kept, the one I don't even let myself open and read. Veronica is on the cover talking to Jughead. She doesn't see Betty and Archie kissing behind her back. I don't tell him about the movie, Chris, or Maya's emoji-only responses when I mention him now.

I surprise myself and write about how empty I felt packing up my room and helping my mom load our ancient blue and white bowls into boxes in the kitchen. Except I don't write *empty*—I write *weird.*

I write about school—about how I'm doing okay in science for now ("we're really into volcanoes this quarter"), better now that I've dropped into Math A ("it feels good to be good again"), and starting *The Great Gatsby* ("the eyes are god, I think").

I want to like Jordan Baker because of her name but I just keep thinking: *What are you doing with these awful people? Get out while you can.* Gatsby waits for Daisy and Nick waits for Gatsby and in the end, it's just a dying green light. No one waits for Jordan.

STILL SEPTEMBER 24TH

In the group text—
Have you heard anything from him? Andrea texts.

From me: a frown, a dot dot dot.

Leslie's at her boyfriend's and I'm sitting in the hall with Peanut outside her bedroom door after school.

If you do, let me know, Andrea texts.

Same, Leslie texts. A heart.

Maya sends me a quiz to take, this one about what superpower you should have. I already know I want the answer to be *flight,*

but I get *invisibility* instead.

In the past I would've wanted that, but now something in me would rather get up and go, go anywhere, than disappear.

I guess my answers don't match my brain,
or my brain isn't ready for my answers.

THE OTHER THING

I still haven't sent more pages of the book.

He's stuck somewhere in the middle and I'm near the end, so we can't talk about what I think is going to happen.

But we can't talk now anyway, I guess.

I text Maya about it because it feels like too much to tell Chris. Maya already knows how this goes. My anxiety. The waiting.

Everything on prison terms.

The phone ringing.

And not ringing.

"You forgot again?" my mom asks. "I left the stamps and envelopes on the counter." I've seen them there every morning and night since the moving sale.

I bring dinner on plastic plates over to the couch.

"I just forgot," I say.

She says my name. "Why aren't you sending him more of the book?" Instead of answering her, I turn on the TV. She sits down beside me.

"Are you mad at me? Are you mad at him?" she asks.

I shrug. The answer is both. But mostly I'm mad at myself. Mad that October is coming and I don't feel ready to be out of our house.

I'm mad at the house too.

Mad that I can't say I'm angry, mad *that* I'm so angry, and it's not one thing. My anger is nameless. For so long, the house was alive with his voice and his moods and now I can't hear him out loud, so he lives in my head—

and I don't know what I'm waiting for. If it's something worse.

Or the guilt of wanting something better.

"If I were you," I say quietly, "I wouldn't even talk to him anymore."

The last time he called, there were things each of them wanted to say to the other. Instead, they said those things to me.

Selfish.

Abandonment.

Delusional.

But I miss him.

Honeybee, I did it all for our family.

"So you're not mad?" she asks.

"No," I say, not telling her she's asking the wrong questions.

I want to ask her why she waited until it was all up to someone else, like the court, like the judge, like the guards I see in my nightmares—

to let him go, to choose us instead.

To choose me.

"Jiord," she says, pausing to bite her chicken, "there's not that much of the book left. Once you send the rest, that's it."

"I know," I say, forking a piece of broccoli. "That's kind of how books work. You read them and then they're over."

She sighs. I chew.

"Do you want me to tear the pages out for you?" she asks.

"No." I look at her. "Why would you do that?"

She throws her hands up. "Just . . . if you wanted me to."

"I can do it myself," I say, turning the volume up.

"*Good*," she says, louder, "because I think you should send him the rest."

I put my leftover broccoli on her plate.
She always gives me too much.

SEPTEMBER 25TH

Before the bus comes,
I stick a thick handful of pages in an envelope,
press a stamp on the front,
put it in the mailbox at the bottom of our hill,
and flip its red flag.

This is the chapter where he finds out whether
Matt's going to make it or not.

It'll take several days, but when he gets it,
he'll read all the pages in one sitting.

In the cafeteria, Britt lets me cut in line.
It's tacos today. "How's it *going*?" she says,
putting two on her tray.

"Feels like it's been forever," she says.
She's wearing a teal cropped cardigan
and heeled sneakers. Effortlessly cool.

"It has," I say, probably more eager
than I mean to be. "How's school for you?"

"Oh you *know*," she says.

I know she has an honors bio class
with Noelle—I ask how that is.

We talk for a couple of minutes
and she tells me, "Hey, Noelle did tell me
about your dad." She waves at someone

passing by. "Hope that's okay."

I feel myself get hot, but
I'm surprised I feel
more relieved than annoyed.

Like maybe Noelle knew.
A friend to a former friend—
not gossip.

I don't talk to Maya or Noelle
about Britt, that I miss being friends,
real friends.

Maya didn't know Britt
when Britt and I were close.

Maya went to a different school then.

I tell Britt, "That's okay. Yeah."
But we both go quiet.

Before Britt,
I'd never lost a friend who hadn't
moved away.

We never talked about her being
Black or me being white.

I didn't know how.
I don't know if Britt did either.
I didn't know we needed to.

And then I met Maya.
We got closer and it was easy.
I let Britt go.

Now I take a chance. I say,
"Do you want to talk sometime?"

She nods. She says, "For *sure*."

"That's why I feel bad—
for not sending them sooner," I tell Maya
at our lunch table.

We're early, both of us with lunch from home,
waiting for Noelle to filter in
from the hallway outside the cafeteria.

Catelyn is sitting at another table
and she waves to us. The waving isn't forced,
which makes it somehow weirder.

To me, but not to Maya, who reminds me
that Catelyn's house is super nice.
Cate's house.

"I spend ten minutes putting it together
and it takes my dad less time than that to read it."

"Uh-huh," she says.

"Do you think I should just send the rest
all at once?" I ask, pulling my egg salad sandwich
out of its plastic wrapping.

"I don't know," she says. "I mean."

I stare at her.

"You're not going to do this book thing again,
are you?" she says, looking around.
"So, I think, yeah . . . send the rest all together."

I haven't told her
I'm not planning to send another book,
so I don't know why she assumes as much.

Or why it bothers me.

Noelle sits down next to me. I decide
not to tell her what Britt told me—
it got us talking again, *maybe.*

"What are we talking about?" Noelle asks,
removing a tube of concealer
and an orange from the same backpack pocket.

I open my mouth
and Maya says, "I'm going to get a bag of chips,"
and heads to the other side of the cafeteria.

"We were talking about my dad," I say, dejected.

"Oh," Noelle says, pursing her lips.
"How's that going?" She leans in
as if I have gossip.

"By 'that' do you mean my dad?" I snap.

Noelle looks embarrassed.
She leans under the table
to comb through her backpack for something.

"Sorry," she says, resurfacing with a tiny mirror.
She pats my hand like you would a child's.
"I really do want to know."

I tell her about not hearing from him,
the book, its missing pages,
and ask her whether I should just send the rest
and be done with it.

Will my dad be upset or offended
if I go from sending some, to none, to all of it
at once?

I haven't finished the book for myself yet,
but I'm near the end. I know enough to know
that part of being the hero, for Matt,

is never giving up. At times,
he's an outcast, he's even *hunted,*
and I don't know if he'll ever truly be free

of his past. But I like reading about his fight
for a future.

Maya comes back mid-sentence and sits down
without a word.

She puts a bag of chips into her backpack
and opens a can of soda.

When I finish talking,
Noelle blurts, "You should do it."

She dabs dots of concealer under both eyes
and on her chin. Staring into her mirror,
she says, "Send him the rest of the book."

Maya doesn't look at me when she says,
"That's exactly what I said."

"Don't you think he wants to know
how it's going to end?" Noelle adds, surprised.

I raise an eyebrow. *Obviously*.

"What I *mean*," she says, drawing out the words,
"is if someone couldn't send me a whole book
so they sent me ten pages a week
or a month or whatever, I'd lose my mind."

She looks at me sideways, cheeks sucked in,
like her brain's just caught up with her mouth.

All I wanted was for someone to tell me
what to do
and why, in case it's the right thing.

I wanted someone else to do the deciding.
To tell me who and how to be.

But no matter what anyone says or does,
I still have to do the living.

"Yeah. You're right," I say.
Her mouth relaxes into a smile.

I thought my dad wanted to be surprised
by the story, but now I think,
He only wants to keep me around.

Maya cups her chin with her palm,
rocking to one side.

She says, "Can we talk about something else?
Like what are we doing this weekend?"

We talk about other things, normal things,
like the bad haircut
someone in Maya's Italian class just got

and this one guy in band Noelle
likes now who seems to like her too,
but who *knows.*

She asks me about Chris,
who I made plans with this weekend—

"But you're moving in like a week,"
Maya says. "I thought maybe . . .
you'd want to hang out with *us,*

just get your mind off of things."
I notice how she says *us*, like
us versus them. Us versus *him*.

I say totally, I would, I still could,

but I told Chris I'd go to his house
to watch an old movie he loves
that I've never seen

and when I tell them what it's about—
mobsters, a doomed romance—
Maya says, "Cool. Cool."

SEPTEMBER 26TH

When the phone
rings
after school,
I'm home
alone
and
unprepared.

WHAT HAPPENED

While he's talking, I can't explain it, it happens

like this.

I hear some words and not others. My ears burn.

My heart bangs against my rib cage like a trapped animal
trying to force an exit,

my dad explaining in slow, low words that

there was a fight and

his *nose was broken* and

he was *put in solitary for a week* and

he's *okay now* and—

all I see when I open and shut my eyes
is static, like on an old TV,

and I feel a cramp forming in my stomach,

like I'm paddling

and I'm paddling and I look and

the shore

is gone.

SHOCK

I lie down
on the floor
I shake
in my room
like I'm
dying
like I'm
playing dead
like I'm
playing myself
in a movie
all I see is
my dad
in a box
alone
the hours
hours passing
the bruises
all I see is
blood and the pain
how painful
is it
I squeeze
the bridge
of my nose
all I see is
someone broke
his nose

they broke
his nose
and left him
alone
and Peanut
paws at my legs
I'm sorry girl
I just can't
get up
I just—

WHEN SHE WALKS IN THE DOOR

at six, I get off the floor. I tell my mom what he told me and she lets out a sob, her elbows hitting the kitchen counter with such force that Peanut jumps back from us and retreats beneath the kitchen table, unsure of her place in all this.

"Can you STOP," I say, clenching both fists at my sides.

She stares at me, both of us surprised.

"I'm sorry I'm *upset*," she says, slapping her hands down, a crying jag building. It makes me angrier. "Can't I have feelings too? He's my *husband*."

"*Yeah?*" I say, before I can stop myself. "Well, thanks to you, he's my *dad*."

It's like someone uncurled a garden hose and started blasting everything in sight. But I don't care. I want to hurt her, like they hurt me.

"It was bad before," I say. "Now I have to think about *this* happening every day? Worry about this *every day*."
She doesn't say anything.
"You picked him and he didn't pick us and we still have to deal with this!"

"I can't believe," I say, each word followed by an invisible period, "this is our life."

I don't realize I'm crying until I'm in my room, the door between us like a brick wall. I hear Peanut sniffing at my door and I let her in, the last living creature I can trust.

WHEN WE USED TO PRACTICE

jujitsu
at home,
I remember
wanting
to give up,
thinking
on my feet,
wanting not
to block
his fist,
wanting
to let it
connect—
crack
against
my cheek,
like
the first bite
of an apple,
wanting
my hurt
to show
like
a bruise,

thinking
he wanted
to win
at any cost,
thinking
I was
the cost,
thinking
let him,
thinking,
let me.

WITH AND WITHOUT YOU

THE LAST TIME

we ever drive down the hill from our house,
it becomes our first house,
a shadow box with no one inside.

My mom looking back in the rearview mirror,
ahead to our next house,
our next life.

Every second down the driveway I want
to be back in my room
with the door shut,

writing in my notebook—poems about leaving,
poems about wanting to sink deeper
or just float away.

The first night in my new room, it's quiet—
no music, no ghosts. Just my pile of boxes,
my blank walls, and me.

THE NEW HOUSE IS A GOOD PLACE TO HIDE

The windows in my room cranked open over my bed, a false summer outside, texts from Maya and Chris asking

how it's going and *are you ready to hang out*

after canceling on them both after the call, before the move, and I tell Maya *soon* and Chris *yes* and Chris and I go to the playground at my old school and sway on the swings for hours and we listen to specific songs on repeat on his phone,

this one that I like about a city with no children in it
because it makes me feel like we're living in the *after*—

that that was *that* and I never have to *go back to that.*

Chris tells me about going to church camp when he was younger, where he learned to tie different knots. He says he let a blond boy kiss him in the woods during a game. He says, *It didn't feel like anything, but he was nice.* I like that he doesn't look away when he tells me this. I like that he twirls a strand of my own dark hair, dark like his, as he says *blond.*

He tells me about playing soccer and wanting to learn to play the guitar but never getting one for Christmas or his birthday. I say, *I want to get better at piano. I have my dad's keyboard.* He asks if I'll play him something, but I say I don't remember how to play any songs.

I end up telling him, *I've never dated anyone,* and he says, *I wouldn't have known,* and I say, *Thanks?* and I ask to wear his watch, which is too big, and I see it's time to go home for dinner. And the sinking feeling, how it means I know, I know I like him.

OCTOBER 6TH

I sit on Leslie's bed while she unpacks more boxes,
Peanut sandwiched between my feet,
eyes wide open and watching.
She pulls out a blue sweater with a wide neck,
a rolled-up poster, a notebook, a bunch of loose pens.
The built-in drawers in her room stick,
like they need to be oiled.
I've given up unpacking for now,
my bedroom downstairs a lot smaller than my old one,
right off the kitchen. The house might be smaller,
but it *is* quieter with my dad gone, just my mom
and Leslie and me here. Andrea came over to help
with the move, and we all ate pizza.
When the phone rang, we all talked to my dad,
a quick minute
here and there, a line about the house,
how it's good, we're good, hope he's good,
We'll finally get to see you this weekend,
it's been so long,
and I thought,
how strange that we have the same number,
the same phone, the same cord stuck in a new wall.

I'M AFRAID

to visit my dad in prison.

Afraid of the drive and the anticipation,

the waiting,

and the sounds and the guards.

Afraid to see my dad in his jumpsuit.

Afraid of the other visitors

and their faces,

our every sadness, thick like molasses

in the air.

This part of the story will never change.

I wish it could.

OCTOBER 7TH

Maya has a project for her photography class, the class with the teacher who played nothing but Death Cab for Cutie on repeat each period—until someone stole her whole huge binder of CDs and none of us knew whether it was jealousy or boredom or if they just really hated Death Cab.

"Yeah, she's not getting those back," Maya says, cutting a prepackaged roll of mozzarella and prosciutto into thin slabs on a plate for me in her kitchen.

I'm her model this afternoon, wearing her flowy floral dress that looks like it's from the '70s and a cardboard sign we made that says

ANYWHERE BUT HERE

in thick black marker.

I think her theme is leaving. Or maybe dissatisfaction.

I pose around the backyard, cupping a flower, trying to look cool and distant in a pair of oversize sunglasses, my hair falling thick and semi-straight like a magazine hippie, as intended.

She pauses to look at the different shots periodically and moves me around to test the lighting. "I feel like I never see you anymore," she says while I'm distracted, moving into my next position.

"You're seeing me right now," I say, as we stand on her porch for more photos. I know it's a mistake as soon as the words are out.

She contorts my arms and leans me lazily against the front door. "You're always with Chris or talking about Chris. I get it, I totally get it, but it sucks too." She shrugs.

I put my hands up, like *Whoa.* We've been on a handful of dates. *Though we do text all the time.* "Maya, it's been like ten seconds of Chris."

Neither of us says anything. "I'm not jealous," she says. "But I'm not *not* jealous, I guess."

"Maya, I'm not *always* with anyone," I say, annoyed. I feel like I could cry, which makes me angry. With Maya and with myself. "It's been really hard."

She looks away. "I know. Sorry, okay? But even if you're not with him, you're texting him or talking about him or whatever."
My phone makes a sound, as if on cue.
"See?" she says.

"That's *him* texting *me!*" I say.

She says, *Come on,* and I say, *I hear you,* that I'll make more time for her.

"Maybe we can do something as a group?" I suggest. It's not a no, it's a sure, why not.

When I tell her about visiting my dad this weekend, the long drive with my mom, she asks if I want to borrow any CDs and I don't tell her that Chris has already made me a mix.

We sit at her computer for a couple of hours, switching off who does what, each of us blowing things up and steering us into quizzes about our soul mates and which characters in different Disney movies we are. Our answers are never the same.

OCTOBER 9TH

It's my first time at Chris's house,
first time meeting his parents
before they leave for dinner,
dressed up like a holiday card.
They both hug me, his dad says
he's heard *so much about me,*
while Chris looks embarrassed, but
fake embarrassed,
like he wants me to know
he's told them about me.
Don't hang out in your room
and *We'll be back soon,*
Chris's mom says awkwardly,
but politely, softly,
and he says, *Goodbye*
and waves them out the door.
I think it's sweet, even if
I don't think
my mom would think twice
about a bedroom door closed
in our house
with a boy inside.
His house is like a postcard
for a bed and breakfast.
Cloaked in trees and somehow
still sunny.

He shows me around the house,
where I learn his parents
keep a bottle of vodka
in the fridge
and long, sharp knives
in a block on the granite counter
of the kitchen island.
I always think kitchen islands
are for rich people
in rich houses.
Or for *comfortable* people
in *comfortable* houses.
Bottles of wine, basil growing
on the windowsill.
Books stacked horizontally
on shelves in the hall,
a small marble bust of Jesus
with his thorny crown,
at least I think it's Jesus—
Chris shows me these things
in passing
and then his room,
where his jeans hang in the closet
instead of folded in drawers
and he has a poster of *Annie Hall,*
which he thinks is better
than *Manhattan,* though
I haven't seen either.
In his desk drawer,
he has a bunch of books

of matches from different restaurants.
He says he collects them,
but he never uses them.
There's a tube of
black liquid eyeliner in there too
and I ask if he ever uses it
and he says sometimes.
Can I put it on you? I ask
and he smiles. He says okay
and he sits for me at his desk,
eyes closed. I take longer
than I need to, watching his
face as I trace his upper lids
with the eyeliner,
nervous, happy, trying
not to move too fast.

And then we watch *The Godfather*
in the living room
and kiss and kiss
and he says it's his favorite movie
and I don't know why,
but I like the way everyone
seems to hate everyone else
out in the open,
every look as loaded
as a line of dialogue.
Hard to believe
tomorrow I'll be
on the long drive

to see my dad
in a jumpsuit, in a crowd,
in a locked room, a thought
that turns to sand
in my mind,
dense at first and then
disintegrating into nothing
I can see.

AM I SCARED TO GO?

Chris asks and I say yes, I am, and I'm
scared like a kid
in a dark movie theater—

I used to sit with my legs crossed
in my seat, thinking ghosts
or bugs or something I couldn't imagine

was below, waiting to get me,
waiting for me to let my guard down,
so I never let my guard down, I say,

tracing the beauty mark on his forearm
like a punctuation point,
like the end of a sad song

I'm afraid I'll never stop singing.

THE DRIVE

should take four hours,
but it takes six with stops and traffic.
That's why we leave Saturday morning
for a Sunday visit that starts
at noon.
"Thank you for doing this," my mom says
to Leslie and me.
"Of course," Leslie says.
Andrea had to work,
will come with us next time.
Next time.
"I love him too," I say flatly,
like I'm resting my case
against myself.
But the words are really more like
I'm a good person
when I repeat them in my head.
Leslie plays DJ in the passenger seat,
switching over to Rufus Wainwright,
the volume loud enough
that the music temporarily fills
my head with lyrics, only lyrics.
The wind picks up
and thin trees shake around us,
each one
redder and more golden than I expected.
I zip up my hoodie.
At a rest stop,

we all eat cold turkey sandwiches
out of plastic containers
on a bench.
My mom holds our hands,
seated between us, her left wrist
sparkling in the light, there—
a thin gold monogrammed bracelet
that belonged to her dad.
We face our blue car
parked between
two white ones,
one of which is completely covered
in bird shit.
I point and say that's how I feel
and we all laugh, which is something.

AT THE HOTEL I FINISH
THE HOUSE OF THE SCORPION

while my mom reads in the other bed beside us,
hers a political thriller that takes place in a different time.

In my book, the evil lord dies,
like I wanted him to. But almost everyone else dies too,

and then Matt takes over the country left behind—
a country with no one to keep him company.

It's a lonely conclusion, but hopeful.
A dark beginning.

"How was it?" my mom asks,
looking up from her book, her thumb keeping it open.

"It had kind of a sad ending," I say.

"Oh," she says, a frown forming. "I'm sorry."

"No," I say, "It was sad, but it was right."

Leslie shares a bed with me, even though I roll in my sleep.
She texts for a while and then reads the book she brought—

it's poetry. I read a few sections over her shoulder.
Something about a *quiet world.* I like it.

We fall asleep to the TV, the volume way down,
a sleep timer counting down until

we're just shapes in the pitch black,
far from home.

THE VISIT

We wait our turn to be called.

We put keys, rings, and bags on a conveyor belt, just like at the airport. They pat us down, give us back some of our things. We're allowed to bring one clear bag with change for the vending machine.

My mom brought a plastic bag full of too many quarters and dollar bills, just in case.

Security guards take small groups up to the second floor, where we wait to be let into the big, rundown visiting room. Once inside, we pick three seats by the window, against the far wall.

When the guards let them out, it's a sea of slow-motion orange and khaki jumpsuits.

My dad walks over to us, familiar and not. His face is sallow and freckled, more freckled maybe. We hug for the allowed time—somewhere between five and ten seconds.

There are no signs posted, but the arbitrary time limit is enforced. If someone lingers, a guard yells out. It's embarrassing for everyone.

It's a social construct, my dad says, like so much of prison life is, even this: the time it takes to greet a person.

We can sit together, but we aren't supposed to touch.

He tells us more about the prison library and playing guitar, and how he's been helping prisoners working toward a GED.

He tells us about a prisoner known for his temper—

a man who says very little, *beats the shit out of most guys for no reason at all*—

who asked for help writing a card to a daughter he'd never met.

"He asked me how to spell 'birthday,'" my dad says, his eyes glossy. "Birthday."

My mom holds his hand, briefly, eyes glued to his face. She listens intently. She tells him that he looks good. Since the move, she's sounded tender on the phone with him. Softer, like you might talk to a child. If ever she mentions divorce to me lately, she flip-flops so sometimes it's only about the finances, the legal stuff, and not about their marriage—or us as a family. It's complicated, she says, not meeting my eyes. I can't tell what's love and what's sympathy, if she misses the husband she says she used to have. The dad I can barely remember.

I can feel Leslie's thigh pressing against mine. Or mine pressing into hers.

I scan the room. The walls are a murky shade of white, a dusty eggshell, the tiles worn and cracked beneath my feet. Long fat fluorescent tubes of light hang above us,

threatening to break.

I can count on one hand the number of teenagers here.

White teenagers, even fewer.

I get up to get my dad a drink: he requests Crystal Light pink lemonade, a recent favorite, he says. The commissary doesn't have it but it's here in the vending machine.

I hear my dad makes less than a dollar an hour from working in the library and doing labor outside.

I can't do the math on what will be his to take home by the end of his time—

because in some sense, it doesn't matter.

Because he'll still owe victims,
victims I don't know.
How much, I don't know.

Because my mom will be paying for us
on her own.

I fumble with the plastic bag at the vending machine. My hands shake like I'm on a sugar high. A guard to my left watches me. He watches as I insert four quarters and drop the fifth.

I turn to watch as it rolls on its side, a gray speck spinning away from me. It stops against a pair of worn off-white sneakers—
the same pair my dad has. But these have no laces.

He is six feet tall, dark and muscular, dressed in orange, holding my quarter in his fist, just out of reach.

As his hand lowers to my open palm, I see the guard tense.

He never looks at me. He only stares at the man in orange. A look I can't describe.

This yours? the man asks me. I nod. A half smile.

This moment feels infinite. But he hands me the quarter, his fingertips calloused, and it's over.

I put the final quarter in the machine, my pulse thumping in my ears. I don't know whether I should be afraid of anything in this room, just that I am—that the fear is rooted somewhere in the guard's gaze. All the things we can see without saying. Think without asking.

I carry the bubblegum-pink plastic bottle back to my dad, silent.

Leslie, hair wisping around her face, the point of her chin. I focus on these things. I see her, she sees me. I try to imagine what's in her head, but all I get is a memory, and barely that—a flicker of a scene in my mind of the time we played library in her room as kids and she stamped my book, which was her book, on loan to me.

Behind my dad, there's a couple of men with beautiful women and screaming babies bouncing on their knees. One of the women wears gold bangles and long braids. The other has on a green sweatshirt with the hood and front pocket cut off.

A boy a little younger than me ignores a loud argument between a prisoner and the woman visiting him.

He's on an old Game Boy. I didn't think those were allowed in here.

My dad's shoes have shoelaces threaded across the tongue—because he wasn't convicted for physically harming anyone, because he's not on suicide watch.

He has shoelaces because he likes to exercise when he can,
walk the track outside, find the biggest space in
his world,
and spend his minutes there.

His jumpsuit is khaki.

He didn't have shoelaces when he first got here, the idea being that he might use them as a weapon against other prisoners. Or against himself.

Prison leaves you only so many choices, he wrote me in a letter.
What you do or don't do with your shoelaces
is one of them.

He tells us more about playing guitar with some men in their downtime in the rec room, men who call him *Maestro*. His guitar has only three strings, he says.

"It's harder to play for people that way,"
he explains, "but if you're good, you're good."

This is because sometimes other prisoners use the guitar strings for tattooing, draining ink from pens and practicing on themselves—the backs of thighs, shoulders . . . whatever's handy. My dad doesn't want one, although he says some of the men offer to pay him for guitar lessons in ink.

The man from the vending machine is somewhere in the orange row, with a toddler on his lap and a couple of adults seated across from him. When he laughs, his face looks wide open, a window into a parallel universe.

I wonder why he's here.

I wonder if my dad knows, but the question doesn't feel like mine to ask.

When visiting hours end, after my mom has nodded her head off and worn her smile thin, we all stand up to say goodbye. Like statues coming to life.

When my dad hugs my mom for longer than allowed, a guard behind him says, "Get off of her." Like he's talking to a wild animal. A cold instruction.

And then   in a move no one saw coming,

                    my mom says, *Fuck you* to the guard at my dad's back.

No one hears her but the guard and us. How smoothly disgusted she sounds, and how prepared. How I wish I'd known this woman, how I wish that anger had another place to go.

The guard doesn't say anything, which surprises me. He turns his face away. But I see how he smirks, like he's better than this moment. Than us. Like he doesn't care.

And I wonder if he would've reacted, would've done something—said something, maybe taken it out on my dad after the fact—if we weren't one of the only white families here. Not all the guards are white, but this guard is.

Before he's led away from us, my dad asks if I want the rest of his drink. It's nearly empty in his hand, that nauseating pink color not found in nature. I say no—*I want you to have it.*

Still watching, the *fuck you* guard tells him he has to leave it behind.

ON THE DRIVE HOME

We listen to Counting Crows, we eat the granola bars
and peppermints my mom has in the glove compartment,
we *decompress,* as she says.

My mom's friend Sarah calls her and she puts it
on speaker, Leslie holding the phone while my mom
yells into it, *Hey! How are you!* in ultimate cheer mode.

There's a *fake it 'til you make it* quality
to my mom's optimism that feels important to appreciate,
but in the moment, I just want to sleep.

Leslie and I cringe as the two of them are louder
than they need to be—*we can hear them, they can hear
each other,* I mouth to Leslie, and she nods vigorously.

When the call ends, we turn the music back up
and my mom sings along extra loud. We *decompress.*
I think of Maya's mom's "me time" and smile. I text her.

Leslie asks when she'll get to meet Chris
and my mom perks up, they both want to meet him—
I should invite him over for dinner.

And it's not that I'm ashamed of the new house,
the house is fine, but picturing that marble bust of
maybe Jesus, I wonder what Chris will think.

OCTOBER 12TH

Chris comes for dinner and we order ______.
I told him to wear whatever, it's just

weeknight dinner at my house,
but he shows up in a ______ shirt and

nice black pants. A restaurant outfit,
if ever I've seen one. My mom gives him

a big hug and says, "It's so great to finally
meet you!" Leslie hugs him too

and he looks ______. I notice that he looks
good in my house, good like *right,*

good like ______. We sit at the table and
talk about ______, especially because

Leslie studied it last year and she loved
reading ______. He seems stiff, ______,

but glad to be here. Leslie texts me
after dinner that she likes him

and a ______ emoji. *Was he wearing
eyeliner?* she asks. I look at him

in my room, his fingers going over
the spines of my books, like he's

searching for ______. *Oh yeah!* I text,
I guess so with a little winking

face. And she texts back,
______ *cool.* He goes home late

and I go into my mom's room,
where she's on the phone with journal

friend. She smiles when she hangs up,
tells me, "Jiord, he's ______."

NEXT: CHRIS AND MAYA

I manage to get Maya and Chris together for lunch.
I don't know how this will go,
but Maya and I split two specialty slices of pizza

and that part feels normal, like always.

"You didn't tell me about your mom," Maya says,
jabbing the air with her plastic knife.
"Go, Kathy. She *would* tell that guard to fuck off."

I laugh.

"I wish I'd seen it," she says.

Chris shifts in his chair,
twisting the straw around in my soda.

There's a silence I fill with details about each of them—

"Maya takes great photos
and I get to model for her in exchange for snacks after school"

and "Chris is going to Prague this winter with his dad
and taking a gender studies class"—

but it doesn't work.

Maya makes a face at the gender studies part,
like *of course,*

and Chris pretends he doesn't see, but I know he does.

He asks what kind of camera she uses
because he has a Nikon *something something,* and when she explains
that they're making DIY pinhole cameras with shoeboxes in class,

he doesn't ask any more questions.

I'm suddenly very aware of the couple of years between Chris and
me.

I glance at his watch and tell Maya we should go
or Chris and I are going to be late.

For what, I don't know. And she doesn't ask.

THE LAST PAGES

I stack, fold, and put them in the mail
to my dad. The end of the book
all over again for me.
I tell Leslie about the friction between
Maya and Chris, how Maya said Chris was
kind of weird, okay? and Chris said Maya was
fine and she says that kind of thing happens,
that it can be hard when you have a boyfriend
and your friend doesn't, and vice versa.
But I don't know if that's it
or if it was the Nikon *something something*
and Maya's eyes glazing over when Chris mentioned
a German movie he wanted to see
at the independent theater, the one
with the tiny chocolate Bundt cakes I like.
Leslie says, *Maybe it's both.* She pulls out a bag
of chips and we eat handfuls together standing
in the kitchen
and I feel better. Enough so that when my dad calls,
and I answer, and it's noisy in the background and he says
it's *nothing, it's just that time,*
a lot of phone traffic in the evening, my stomach
doesn't double knot. But I also wonder
if he would prefer we forget these details, ignore them,
or if he wishes, secretly, that we could be there
with him, a witness. That any of us, or all of us,
could. I don't think he thinks about
how old I am or who I am

to him when he tells me things
about his days or the nights there.
He tells me about walking the track outside,
the color of the sky, how it's getting colder
but the clothes aren't getting any thicker,
that it was a decent day, and then
about a new prisoner who's too young to be there,
who gambled his student loan money away.
I say it's terrible because it is,
but I also say *lots of things are terrible,*
and let the words hang there,
my voice gruff in a way
that feels new
and a little terrible too. I ask
if he has time to talk to Leslie and he says
he has to go but *tell her I love her* and I shake my head
at her and I pace and I watch myself
in the hall mirror on the phone,
my narrowed eyes, the hard line of my mouth,
and I feel like
whoever she is, I could love her,
one day.

OCTOBER 16TH

October is my favorite month
because the days gets cooler,
the nights darker
and infinite—
because Halloween means
costumes, chocolate-covered everything,
apple cider, badly carved pumpkins,
and watching not-horror
horror movies with my friends,
dressing poor Peanut like a pumpkin
for all of five minutes
before she shakes the stem from her head,
her face crinkled further like,
What did I ever do to deserve this?

Maya comes over after school
and we do homework
in the living room
with cheese and crackers
and on in the background is a Lifetime movie
where a group of teenage girls make a pact
to get pregnant together,
which makes us laugh even though
it's not funny. We can't look away.

Noelle texts us about having a party
Halloween weekend ("!!!")—
her older brother having his friends over,

their parents out of town,
a bottle of SKYY vodka someone's sister
promised to buy—
and I can't concentrate
on supervolcanoes for tomorrow's quiz,
which are the most dangerous type,
my notes say.

In theory, it's like this:
a whole magma chamber erupts,
creating a hole
into which everything collapses,
changing life as we know it.
No one knows—and this part I underlined
three times—
when the next one will be.

HAVE TO

For dinner my mom, Leslie, and I have
rotisserie chicken, wild rice,
and asparagus. These chickens are frequent,
they're buy-one-get-one-free
at Costco,
just like the ice cream in our freezer,
the on-sale jumbo boxes of gummy fruit snacks
in the cabinets.

There was a time my parents would get dressed up
and go out for dinner, like Chris's parents—
I can smell my dad's cologne, hear my mom's
bracelets clink together in the hall, then
out through the garage door,
gone, gone together
like a matching set.

We had rotisserie chickens then too.
The difference is that we didn't have to.

AT NIGHT

my dad calls
and spends most of his minutes on
my mom, and when it gets to me,
she pushes the phone into my hand

and goes to her room,
like, *You deal with it,* and he sounds
agitated, so I'm agitated,
and he says, *I feel like you're forgetting*

me. I suck in a breath and say
I'm sorry I haven't written since the visit,
I've been busy with everything,
you know? He says he's just missing

us, he says, *Your MOTHER,* he says
he didn't sleep last night. I dig
my fingernails into my free
forearm until red half-moons form.

He read the pages I sent—he liked
the end of the book. *What's next?*
I wonder that for myself.
I say I don't know yet.

I text Chris and ask if he's free to talk
because *I'm upset, my dad,*
and he says *I would ♥,*
but he's hanging out with a friend.

He says he'll call me later,
but then it's later and he doesn't.

POEM FROM FUTURE ME

What are you waiting for,
honeybee, it's going to be you
or it's going to be
me

OCTOBER 17TH

My phone buzzes in my pocket and when I take it out,
it's Chris asking, "How was the QUIZ?"

I write "explosive" and he sends back a skull. I ask if he wants to go with me to the Halloween party and he says, "Do I have to wear a costume?"

I send back ". . . I guess not," and he says he'll go.
I wonder if he thinks dressing up is dumb.

Or childish.

Noelle is waiting for me at my locker,
trying to make space in her backpack by pulling out all the textbooks

and rearranging them in such a way that they still don't all fit,
but differently.

"You're so lucky," she says, "that you dropped precalc. Today *sucked.*"

"Uh-huh," I say. Lucky.

I see Maya down the hall, back to us, talking to Catelyn at what I guess is Catelyn's locker. Catelyn in a baby pink polo. White jeans. Practically bootcut.

"What are you doing later?" Noelle asks, shoehorning her chemistry textbook in between her makeup pouch and *Invisible Man.*

"Wanna go costume shopping after school?" she asks.

"Cool, yeah," I say, "what about—" nodding in Maya's direction.

"Oh, I think she's hanging out with Catelyn," she says, "or something."

I crouch down next to her. "Do you like her?" I ask.

"Catelyn? I mean, yeah, she's nice."

"Church nice or *nice*-nice?" I ask.

"*Jesus* nice," she says solemnly, pushing my shoulder. "No. She's just nice."

"Is she invited to your party?" I ask.

Noelle nods.

"Got it," I say.

But Noelle says, "Catelyn's not Maya's *Jiordan*."

"That's not what I—"

"I know what you mean," she says. "I think Maya thinks Chris is your *Maya* though."

WONDER WOMAN

was originally sculpted from clay and raised as an Amazon,
with superhuman powers gifted by the Greek gods.

At least that's what it says when I google her.

The plastic bag with my costume inside just says:
Transform into woman empowered!

Boot covers, gold cuffs made of foam,
the bodice and the skirt, and the plastic gold headband.

No lasso for truth. But that's okay.

I text Chris about it, and he sends me back star emojis.

Noelle's brother is a year older than Chris, Leslie's age,
and I don't know if he and his friends will wear costumes.

Leslie has a class with Noelle's brother
and they have some friends in common, but no one close.

She's wearing her boyfriend's uniform and going as
a baseball player for Halloween. Out with their friends.

I try to draw Wonder Woman in my black sketchbook,
where I'm supposed to be drawing

homework that won't be checked. Honor system.
Ideas, whatever comes to mind, my teacher says.

I can do the hair and the basic shape,
but when it comes to the face, it's a mystery

trapped in my hands. Leslie could do better.
She could draw the arms, the legs. The lasso.

I erase her legs and try them again and again,
until the faded lines are more obvious

than what remains on the page.

MY MOM CALLS TO ME FROM THE KITCHEN

"It's for you—" she says,
ear pressed to the phone, nodding along
to the recording, and then
pressing a button to accept the call.

It's a different button to block all future calls
from prison. *That* button
is like a grenade inside the phone, always
one quick move away from detonating.

She isn't speaking to my dad right now,
and he tells me, like she told me,
that they had another discussion about
getting divorced. This time,
he says he thinks she should do it to protect herself.

But when I say "That sounds like
a good idea," he says he married my mom because
he wanted to be a father and a husband
and your mom was a nice woman
with two kids, a thing he says

when he wants to make our life smaller,
fit for a window display.
My chest tightens and it's stupid that I ask,
but I still ask, *Didn't you love her?*
a question with only one right answer.
I don't hear whatever he says next.

For the first time, I say *I* have to go.
When I hang up, there are still minutes left,
but I have nothing else to say.

I walk around behind our house,
where a couple of people using walkers
are doing slow loops around the entrance
to the nursing home. I wonder
who loves them
and what their visits are like.

LETTER

Juggling letters and phone calls is complicated because the timing doesn't work out. ______ get lost in translation. So after I watch the walkers outside, I check the mail and there's a letter, my dad's gray block letters penciled on the envelope. His inmate ID, #______, in the top left corner, along with the prison address.

Sometimes I think everyone I know has mistaken me for someone who's learned how to ______ with this.

But I wouldn't know what to ______ me either.

I wait until there's a cotton candy sky outside to read it, after my mom and I eat ______ for dinner, the skin crisp, smelling up the entire house.

He writes: *Honeybee, thank you for sending the rest of the book. I'm so glad that ______ is saved from ______.* He writes that he misses me. That the food is terrible, that he's *exercising like a fiend.* That they watch crappy TV and he bought a couple of ______ at commissary. That he's losing ______. That he feels like he's losing ______. *Do you remember when we went to the ______ as a family?* he writes.

I remember a hay ride and drinking hot chocolate with my sisters. We played ______ and shrieked every time someone made it. There are some memories I want to keep, but I feel those fading too. A lost ______, a language I can't read.

I put the letter in a shoebox with the others. I have the lights ______. I turn on my side, wonder if there's a ______ inside my closet, if this house is ______ too. But I don't get up to check.

There were a lot of good times, I tell Chris when he calls me before bed. "Like one time we went to ______ and my dad ordered ______ and it was so good."

Chris lets out a breath. He asks if it would be better if we didn't talk about *this stuff* as much. "It just seems like it ______ you," he says. "My dad?" I ask. "Yeah," he says. And then he tells me about a band he just discovered online: ______. He says he thinks I'd like them too.

It takes me a long time to fall asleep. When I do, it's dreamless.

______.

THE HALLOWEEN PARTY

Walking through the open gate into Noelle's backyard,
I see her brother's friends on the deck, playing

wildly athletic beer pong, arms sweeping over cups,
a couple of perfectly angled wrists.

Old rap coming out of the speakers, the rhythm
bumping in my chest. Soft and low,

like the night. I can't see the stars.

We stop at the table with bottles, the cooler with cans.
Chris's hand in mine as I take a shot,

then another,

like lighter fluid in my mouth, my throat,
gone—

"It's *so great*," some curly girl in a dark jacket says,
burping her beer, "we got all this." It's her turn.

I've been drunk before in Noelle's backyard
but it was just a few of us girls last year, mostly

playing *Never Have I Ever* and passing around
bottles of hard lemonade,

so sugary I could feel it in my teeth.

Maya calls my name from a group seated
on the trampoline, a net between us—

inside are Catelyn, another girl we know, a couple of boys
from marching band, and someone's hot cousin

dressed like a lumberjack—the scene too heavy,
the trampoline's long legs

fighting gravity in the grass. Up on the deck,
Noelle, a sexy baseball player with a *69* on her chest,

waves from the back door
and stops to hang on one of her brother's friends mid-throw,

sloshing vodka and juice on the wood below.

"We can't fit," I tell Maya, who's dressed like
a beer maid in a plaid skirt and white top,

two long braids hanging still
on the trampoline.

"I'll come out there," she says,
climbing over Catelyn, who's maybe a hippie or

maybe just a kid at summer camp, *I don't care,* I think,
adjusting my cuffs so they stay up on my forearms.

"So cute," says Maya, touching my gold headband.
I hold her braids in both hands, thick and excellent.

"Who did these?" I ask about her hair. "They're amazing."
Catelyn, she says. They met up earlier at Catelyn's house.

I nod. Right.

"And what are you?" she asks Chris,
who looks bewildered, like he can't decide if it's a joke.

But maybe it's me who can't. My face feels hot.
"I told him not to," I say.

"I'm just kidding," she says, then quietly, "*Jesus.*"
Chris half nods in his black V-neck and dark blue jeans,

hands in his pockets. Awkward. I think I love him then,
the look of him, but the vodka has started

to work and I feel light in my body,
like my arms are made of sky, and Maya says to Chris,

"I'll bring her back" and guides me toward the house,
stopping to fill two cups with vodka

and cranberry juice. I feel a stomach cramp beginning,
sitting next to Maya on the brown couch in the den

where I've witnessed Noelle watch hours and hours
of TV while doing homework. I can't do both at once.

How far away I feel from this time last year,
when everything was bad at home but I recognized it,

I knew the shape of my dad's moods,
and Maya was there on the phone or right next to me,

like now, except now

it feels like the space between us is growing,
like we're in a plane going over the ocean

and everything is impossibly small—
I can't hold any of it.

"I just wanted to talk to you for a sec," she says,
gulping her drink,

the backyard visible from the window.

"I get it," I say, before I know what I'm saying.
"You don't like Chris."

I cup my face with my hands. Wait for her.

"Jiordan, I—" she starts, looking around,
"I mean, what do you want me to say?"

Now I'm angry. I can feel the hot tears forming
and I don't want to, no, but maybe I do want to

say what I'm about to say—

"Dude, honestly, what the fuck," I say,
"*I* like him. I don't actually get why you don't."

I rub one of my eyes with my thumb,
taking some glitter eyeshadow with it.

Some superhero I am.

"*Come on*. Seriously," she says.
I raise an eyebrow. Like, *Try me*.

"Fine," she says.
"You want to go there. Let's GO THERE."

"What's your problem?" I say.
"*Is* it just that I don't spend enough time with you?"

Maya stands up so she's towering over me,
which she does by default.

I notice her black stilettos. Mad that I'm impressed
she can walk in those,

I stand up in my flats with the boot covers on,
that much shorter.

"You want to know what my PROBLEM IS?"

It's too late to say I don't.

"YEAH." I stare her down.

She looks like she might cry too, but also
like she hates me, or this moment

when I think we're about to end up
on opposite sides of a fault line.

"HE'S FUCKING PRETENTIOUS AND I HATE HIM."

We look at each other, both stunned,
waiting for something.

A sound.

Anything.

I don't know what to do. I feel like I want to hit her.
I make a fist, I breathe, I try to breathe,

slam my empty cup on the floor, walk past her
like she's a speck,

like she's nothing to me. But I still stop
in the doorway, my back to her.

"Fuck you."

I say it without even turning around.

MISSING

"We. Have. To. *Go*," I say to Chris,
openly crying,
ignoring Catelyn beside him,
my face swollen with it.
I grab his hand like a crutch
and pull him away from the group,
shaking off everyone
in our wake.

I want to break
something with my fingers,
feel something
or someone
pop and shatter beneath me.

I catch Maya's profile in the window
as we pass,
one of her braids behind her left shoulder
shifting up and down,
as if vibrating, and I know she's crying,
and I think, *Good,* and then,
Shit.

WE WALK TO A NEARBY PLAYGROUND IN SILENCE

and I pump my legs harder
and harder on the swings,
until I'm more dizzy than drunk
and the stars overhead look like
planes that will never land,
which I'm telling Chris
instead of the fact that my best friend
hates him because
I don't want to hurt his feelings.
He stands there watching me
for a while
before he asks,
"Really, what happened with Maya?"
and I say, "Just stuff, you know?"
and he says, "But like what stuff?
You can tell me anything."
And I brake with my heels
in the sand below, take his hand,
say, "So the thing is. She doesn't like you
and I don't know what to do."
He nods, expressionless.
"That sucks," he says, "but why do you care
so much what she thinks?"
I don't understand
the question. "She's my best friend,"
I say.

"Do you like *her?*" I ask.
He shrugs. "Not really."
My stomach in my throat
or my heart in my feet,
I feel like I might puke right here
in the sand. My headband slips over
my forehead, covering my eyes.
"I like *you,*" he says,
and it's so quiet
that when I do puke, the sound is like
a wave slapping a wall of rocks
over and over.

ON ACTUAL HALLOWEEN THE NEXT DAY

my mom and I watch *Halloweentown* and I ignore my phone,
which is fine because it turns out no one wants to talk to me

and I don't blame them.

Except for Chris, who seems glad I might not be friends
with Maya anymore. And also not horrified by the puke

or the crying before and after it.

I eat candy corn and bite-size Butterfingers and think about
texting Maya, but it feels impossible. I'm angry.

What did she expect me to do? Break up with Chris?

"Do you think Chris is pretentious?" I ask my mom,
who knows about the fight and told me it would all work out,

that we've been friends for too long for it to end like this—

over a boy. "Of course not," she says. "He's very thoughtful
and smart." She smiles at me. "He's crazy about you."

Something about this makes me feel worse.

Before Leslie left to meet a friend at the park,
she said that it would all work out too.

Things change, she said,
shrugging, gesturing around the house,
like, *Look at us.*

I told her, *Maya was an asshole. But so was I.*

She nodded solemnly.

She said, *Yeah, maybe you were.*

She was wearing a teal sweater and dangly earrings
when she said it, which made her look wise.

My dad calls and I answer it.

Peanut snores loudly, her head resting on my mom's lap,
the movie paused on the grandmother's face, cursed

by the evil force that's overtaken the town.

My dad says he didn't sleep well,
that he's been walking the track, exercising *like a maniac,*

that he can't believe tomorrow is only November.
I nod, *yep,* but he can't see.

He says, "Tell your mother I got her letter."

I tap my foot. I don't ask *what letter.*

He asks if I'm still angry with him,
and I tell him the truth—I don't know how to feel.

AFTER

I tell my mom, *Why do* I *have to talk to him for you,*
and I don't wait for her response.

I go to my room, shut the door, lie down, and let my mind
unravel completely, let myself get shaky

and cry, then get mad at myself for it. Through the door,
my mom says, *Jiord, I'm so sorry*. The words wobble,

like *she* might cry, which makes me angry.
I don't respond.

I don't want to hold their feelings in my chest.
My mind races, looping over bad moments, hard feelings.

I cycle through every stupid thing I've ever said in class,
and the time I wore a black shirt that said *I stop traffic*

in sixth grade and a teacher told me it was inappropriate,

which was kind of funny because my mom picked it out
at T.J. Maxx, or the time I downloaded a game

on the computer I wasn't supposed to

because my dad said it took up too much space
and slowed things down and he was right

but I did it anyway, and how purple his face got,
even after I deleted the game

and lost all the progress I had made.

NEVER TOO LATE

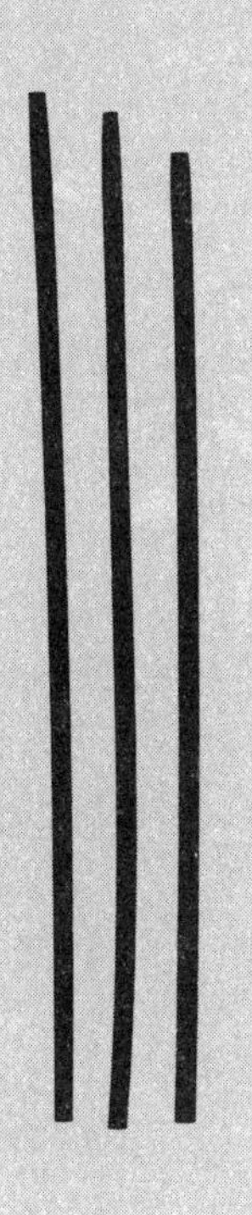

FOR DAYS,

Maya and I exist near each other
but not together.

At lunch, we sit as a group,
but the weirdness is tangible—

I do my homework
and Noelle does her makeup,

Catelyn talks about some show, as if we're an audience,
and Maya doesn't look at me.

I know because
I look at her,

and then away from her

in our math class, where we still sit next to each other
even though there are no assigned seats.

Ryan shows up on Wednesday

but not Monday, Tuesday, or Thursday

and makes fart sounds with his hands instead of
answering the question when he's called on.

This is something
Maya and I would make fun of

if we were friends.

On Friday, Maya opens her mouth
and turns to me,

like she's forgotten that we're fighting.

By now, my anger is softer,
kind of blurry
around the edges.

Scorpions and honeybees only sting
when provoked.

But I still can't say anything,
the distance between us too wide

to cross.

I want to tell her I'm sorry.

I want to tell her that my dad wrote my mom
a flowery letter and now things

seem better with them, which is
confusing.

So I text Chris under my desk and ask
if I can come over later.

SALT AND VINEGAR

"I just miss her," I tell Chris, "that's all."

He takes his arm from behind my shoulders
and starts texting, so I ask, "What would you do?"

He puts his phone face down on the coffee table
and runs a hand through his hair.

We're watching, but also not watching,
a movie with a good soundtrack. And eating chips.

"Don't take this the wrong way," he says, "but
if she doesn't want to be your friend, it's her loss."

I think about what little I know about his friends—
the school ones, who don't live near us,

who he told me he's been close with since
freshman year. And some others, a couple of girls

he's stayed friends with since middle school,
public school. I haven't met any of these friends.

When I don't say anything, he adds,
"You should move on." Each word strangely sharp.

But I never thought it was that Maya
didn't want to be my friend. It's that she did.

It hurts to think about, so I try to ignore it,
focus on the movie, these three brothers

on a train trip to see their mother,
each with their own problems they can't solve.

"I don't think I like these chips,"
I tell Chris. "They hurt my mouth."

"Really?" he says, picking his phone up
again. "They're so good."

He smiles at his screen.

"What is it?" I ask.

I don't realize there's an edge in my voice
until I've said it,

until he puts his phone back down on the table
and says, "Nothing, just a text."

WHEN I GET HOME I CAN'T SHAKE THE FEELING

that Chris is texting someone he might ______. But if I ask I'll seem ______. I text Noelle to ask what she thinks, probably because she'll be the ______, the most ______ about it. She says, "Why don't you just ______ him?" As if it's that simple.

I guess it should be. I want it to be.

I call him late and say, really cool, super calm, "I want to be ______ with you, so if you could just be ______ with me and tell me who you were texting, that would ______. I don't want to feel ______." He laughs, but it's forced. He tells me it's his friend, who's a ______, but she's not ______, he says, and she used to like him, but he never liked her. They've been friends forever and he didn't want me to think anything was ______ so he didn't mention her.

I'm relieved, but then he says, "It *has* been kind of ______ lately, though. Things are just really hard with you." *What.* "I mean *for* you. I want to be there for you, with your ______ stuff, but sometimes it's ______." It's ______ or I'm ______?

"You mean about my dad or Maya? Is it ______?"

______. "It's all of it, I guess."

We're both silent and I feel that familiar ______, a crushing ______. The wind knocked out of my chest.

"I really like you," he says. I say I do too. But when we hang up, I feel like I've given something away, the last ______ I have. ______, like a shooting star.

TEXT TO MAYA, NOVEMBER 10TH

~~Hey, I just want to~~

~~Hey, would you want to maybe~~

~~I'm sorry~~

~~Look, I was super pissed~~

~~I'm still mad, but~~

Hey, can we talk?

OLIVIA ANSWERS THE DOOR

and I walk up to Maya's room like it's the first time, examining each photo on the wall—

Maya as a baby in a legitimate Easter bonnet, Olivia in a Christmas sweater, her mom so young in shoulder pads, and none with Maya's dad, which makes sense. It's only her mom's house now.

All of it: Maya's life before me.

I knock and she answers "Hey" through the door.

Before I even sit down on the floor she says, "Jiordan, I—"

"No, I get it. I was a bitch." The words out. Like throwing a water balloon onto a sidewalk.

She smiles. "Me too."

"I just don't know what to do with you . . . hating Chris."

We're both quiet.

"It was still shitty for me to say what I said." She doesn't say she didn't mean it, which I appreciate.

I tap my nails on the floor, a blob of dark pink nail polish dried there. "Are we still friends?" I ask, picking at it.

"Of course," she says, crossing her legs on the bed. "Maybe you'll hate my next boyfriend." The last time Maya had a boyfriend was in seventh grade, before I knew her. Turns out he went to the same temple as me though. He was nice enough.

"Dude," I say, like *that's not funny*. "That doesn't help."

"I will—we . . . I'll be nicer," she says.

"*Thank* you." I sit next to her on the bed. She shifts to make room.

"We're not always going to like the same things—is what I mean," she says. I nod.

"But you better make time for me," she says. "I was here first."

I lean against her. "You were."

Maya's room, the place I love. And why.

NOVEMBER 13TH

Now when my dad calls
    my mom cradles the phone
against her head
    like it's something
precious,
    like it's someone
precious.
    Every time
she swings
    back and forth with him,
it makes it
    harder for me
to do the same,
    as if the walls of my heart
get harder
    with each smack
in the opposite
    direction.

GOOD ENOUGH

I want to be a good daughter,
but all the love that I still feel for them

as a pair—or used to
and am trying to recapture,

like a moth winging toward a bright light—
doesn't feel like enough.

It feels like dark magic,
something I put on for show.

WAKE UP

I don't want
to write
more poems
from the future.
I don't live
in the future.
I want to feel
myself
right now
in my body,
feel my hands,
feel my notebook,
write this,
this moment,
before the moment
leaves me
behind.

POTENTIAL

Now that Maya and I are good again, lunch is back to normal,
even with Catelyn, who I tell myself I'll be nicer to,
because when she says, *I'm glad you two are talking,*
there's no trace of sarcasm
or jealousy.

What is it about me, I ask Noelle after, that expects there to be?

The bell rings and we're in the hall—
I'm late for Drawing and Painting.

I don't want to finish my painting, I tell Noelle.
If I finish it, it'll be all it can be. The potential is gone.

And it's not great—
a line drawing of a potted plant that turned into
an acrylic hodgepodge of green on green.
No depth. Every leaf looks the same.

"That's okay," she says.

I feel like she's about to give me the perfect pep talk
and—

"It's a painting of a plant. How good could it be?"

NOVEMBER 18TH

In a letter, my dad writes that
when the lights go out,
the contraband cell phones come out.
I like this visual I have
in my head,
like a starry sky. Almost clear,
almost real.
I imagine the scene like
flashlights tenting sheets,
or tiny squares projected
onto a wall
or on the underside of a mattress
above. A lot of it is Facebook,
he says.
Not everything is lost to the system,
I think.
It's easy to forget this
or refuse it.
We don't talk about the fight,
his face, what happened
that led to it, or what happened
to whoever did it.
I can't picture that man.
In my dreams,
my dad is my dad, but also
a figure, fuzzy edged,
that I try to follow
around corner

after corner
but eventually lose
in the dark.
It's the relief
I feel guilty about.
When I round the final corner
and there's no one there.
No one to fear for
and nothing
to be afraid of.

I ALWAYS WANT TO PAUSE THERE

Not wake up.
Not begin again.

I text Chris about the dreams
and he says
at least they aren't
true.

RADIO

He bought a radio at commissary weeks ago
but has yet to put batteries in it.

This is something I like to picture in prison
and it isn't even real—

though it has potential:

my dad
stretching a silver antenna up, up, up

to listen.

AS IF

Hanukkah is early this year, right after Thanksgiving,
which feels so far from winter break

next month, and Christmas Eve
with *It's a Wonderful Life* in black and white,

baby carrots left out for Santa's reindeer, another turkey,
my mom's vat of soup on the stove—traditions

we can afford to keep.

I know money is tight. My mom smiles a fine line
when she says so.

She doesn't complain,

just tells me that the holidays will be *lighter* this year,
and it twists my insides when she says it because

she turns her chin down, as if
she should be ashamed.

As if she hasn't apologized at the mall when I say I like a shirt
and then changed the subject instead of saying, flat out,

I can't buy it.

As if a boy at school asked if I was moving to the nicer
neighborhood, his neighborhood, when he heard I was moving,

and then never talked to me again when I said no.

NOVEMBER 20TH

It's harder to care about having less money
or the girl in class who told everyone
her sweater was more expensive than her friend's—
her own friend's—
because she bought it at Abercrombie
instead of Abercrombie Kids
when I wake up in the middle of the night
with a rock in my stomach, the nightmares dissipating
like paint in a cup of water:

men shouting words I can't make out, my dad
alone on a cot, a siren
blaring . . .
like familiar footage I've seen before in real life,
but spliced and sped up,
with my dad added in, all the color draining
from the scene, his face, my own mind.
That's when I wake up sweating,
watch TV for hours—until my eyes shut, until
my alarm goes off,

and I drag myself through the rest of the day at school.
At lunch, Britt and I talk for a few minutes
and check that we still have
each other's phone numbers saved
before we split off into our separate sides, separate
lives,
and I wish I had whatever it took
to ask her to sit together
like we used to.

AFTER SCHOOL, WE LISTEN TO MUSIC AND TALK

but Chris doesn't want to hear more about my dad—
again he says he thinks talking about it
makes *me* feel bad, but I text Maya
because I'm trying to be more open
about Chris to Maya and Maya to Chris

and she texts, more solemn or mature or something
than I expect, maybe Chris doesn't know
how to deal with it, dot dot dot,
and I text yeah,
that's probably true, dot dot dot—

and I get to thinking, in Chris's bedroom surrounded
by his stuff, that my dad will be gone
for a long time, and if I can't
say what I feel about it
out loud, every which way,
what *can* I say?

NOVEMBER 22ND

At lunch at school,
    we talk about Thanksgiving plans,
        whose uncle gets too drunk
and tells weird stories,
    whose sister is a vegetarian now,
        and why Hanukkah is so early
this year.
    "Does someone tell you when it is?"
        Catelyn asks, and I say, "My mom,
I guess?"
    Noelle asks what I'm getting
        my mom for the holidays
and I say I'm thinking about
    a necklace, something
        long and silver but interesting
and Catelyn asks if I get eight presents
    or one big present for Hanukkah
        and I say it depends
and Noelle says on what
    but Maya shoots her a look
        and I tell Catelyn we celebrate
Christmas and Hanukkah because
    my mom always loved Christmas
        and my dad always had Hanukkah
so I was born into both traditions
    and Catelyn says that's so awesome
        and I say kind of, yeah,
and do basic math

to figure out whether a necklace
is possible or if
I should get to work on a poem
because poems are free
but Maya says we could go
to the bookstore after school
and I think, *Good,*
because like my mom says,
There's always money for books.

DISTRACTIONS

Maya and I get lucky
at the bookstore—
a sale on new paperbacks—

and I get my mom
a book of essays
and a book of poems.

Both feel glossy
in my hands, the way
presents should feel.

After dinner, my dad calls
and talks to my mom,
who nods and says

something sounds *terrifying*
and that
she misses him too,

an expression I can't place
on her hollowed-out face
as she hands the phone

to me. Like an apology.
It's a bad day for him,
I take it,

as he tells me
the psoriasis on his face and arms
has gotten worse

without medication.
There are distractions,
he says,

like making music with the guys.
But during lockdown
the last 48 hours—

this is where my brain
fights itself,
words passing through

without attaching,
like armed guards running down
a hallway—

he says he couldn't go
anywhere, couldn't play music,
couldn't do anything.

If he knows what happened,
he doesn't tell me—
and for that, I'm grateful.

EVERY TIME

I think I'm doing fine,

something happens

with my dad
        with prison
                and I feel   myself

                        tear from

                                myself

                                        until I feel   half alive.

WANT

Standing in my doorway, my mom says she feels helpless
too. Deflated, even.

She sits next to me on my bed, and I want to
not want her there, but it's nice. Nice to not be alone

with my circular thoughts, my horrible, pounding chest.
Nice to be with someone who lives with this too,

like a disease.
Peanut watches us from the floor, cocooned in a blanket.

I ask her when we'll visit my dad again, and she says,
Once a month is just impossible, but doesn't say more.

I'm angry all the time, I tell her, and I feel like
my heart is going to explode

and I'm afraid
of everything, I say, until the words slur together

like a sob lodged in the back of my throat. *I'm sorry*
I get mad at you because you picked him.

I know this isn't all your fault, I say,

waving my arms around at a lot of nothing
but the air between us. *Sometimes I want to disappear,*

I want to be gone, I just want to be gone, I say,
and I don't register the words I'm saying

and then I'm glad I've said them,
even though my mom begins to cry and the sound

is like the trunk of a car slamming shut,
with a living thing inside.

She pulls me into a hug that's too tight
and says, *Please, no,*

you don't—
          you can't—

and we sway back and forth
like a spindly tree giving way to the wind.

You're okay, you're okay, she repeats,
the words rhythmic,

smooth as a stone. But then I realize I don't know
which one of us is the *you* she means.

THE NEXT DAY I DON'T GO TO SCHOOL

My mom and I play hooky—
and we go to the movies.
Maya texts me a heart when I text
It's a mental health day.
We buy popcorn and Swedish Fish,
we sneak into a second one,
we squeeze each other's shoulders
when something wild happens
or something sweet
or something
only the two of us would find funny.
On the drive home she asks
if I feel better, if I'm doing better,
if this helped,
hands tight on the wheel,
and I say today is a good day,
the noise in my head—what if,
what if—tuned to a frequency
I can bear.
I don't need to say
that this is just
another thing
we'll both have to live with.

THE ONE WHERE ___ ___

At 3am, I watch the episode of *Friends* where everyone's late to Thanksgiving dinner. I think about my dad, and what they eat in prison on Thanksgiving—if there are ______, if the ______ are mashed; if there are ______, if the ______ are canned. And the knives: where they're kept, if they go missing, what happens if they go missing. Same goes for forks, spatulas, tongs, spoons. Anything can be ______, brought outside or back to a cell and used to ______ someone. But the day a man broke my dad's nose, he used his hands.

SOMETIMES I WISH

I was back at the family computer in our old house
playing The Sims in my slippers, debating deleting the ladder
from my pretend family's pool just because I could, the parents
fighting over money because I hadn't entered a get-rich-quick
cheat code—

rosebud, motherlode, kaching.

For a long time, I only played fair, only plastic tables, no art on
the walls.
A strict budget before they started making money.
The parents never had a heart-shaped bed or a big TV.
They had an old oven that caught fire
and burned breakfast regularly.
But they survived. They fought. They worked. The daughter went
to school.

Once, several fast-forward months of gameplay later
in a boring blue-brown house on a street with no beginning or
end,

digital mom and dad were in each other's faces, stomping,
yelling about money and how life had disappointed them—
I guess,

because they yelled in Simlish, like English played
backward.

Neither one was watching the daughter doing laps in the early
hours

in the pool before school, becoming a stronger swimmer.

If I paused and deleted the ladder, I knew what would happen—
I'd read articles online:

the girl would bob like an apple, her hands
searching for what's missing. She would get confused, tired,
too tired.

A Sim girl can't just grip the side of the pool and haul herself up.
She wasn't coded that way, or the game wasn't.

Her head would dip low, then bubbles, then
nothing.

A digital urn would pop up on the lawn beside the pool,
a relic of the girl she'd been before.

I was always a boring player.

When I deleted the ladder, I saw her head dip low, then bubbles,

then nothing.

I wanted to bring her back from the dead,
but I let the whole day pass instead, saving the game like a
merciless god,
no going back.

SOMETHING INSTEAD

When my mom asks me if I'm okay,
if I meant what I said about wanting

to disappear,

I say I'm feeling better.

At least I feel like I'm here in my body.
I feel something instead of nothing.

She says she's
always here
if I want to talk.

I wish I had the language for this feeling
of swimming laps
in a frozen lake
as the sun goes down, what it feels like—

how the fear sticks to my ribs
and hardens into something I can't name.

My truth has more thorns than any one word,
even the word *yes.*

Yes can be sharp to the touch.

Like

do I think   my dad is guilty,
  do I think
    I   am guilty,   that my mom is,

that I'm treading water
to get to a destiny
that won't reveal itself to me?

THANKSGIVING

Turkey getting brown
in the oven,
canned cranberry sauce—
the kind I love
that everyone else thinks is
nasty,
that wriggles out
in one big block,
and my mom's classic
creamed sweet potatoes
with marshmallows
broiled on top.
On TV,
the parade is ending
with cheers and a panorama
of pink cheeks.
The final act:
Santa waves to all his fans
there in person, kids
bundled in hats and jackets
rows and rows deep
behind metal blockades
and the cops.
Most of them look content
in the cold, waiting.
I fold napkins while I watch
Santa, who doesn't seem
aware, doesn't seem

to see me here,
in my house,
off camera.
I put out small white
salt and pepper shakers
we've had forever.
If my dad were here tonight,
he'd be grinding pepper
over everything
on his plate.
Once, Andrea added it
to a piece of cake
for him as a joke and
when he tasted it,
I thought he'd explode.
Sometimes
it worked, but
sometimes, the gamble
didn't pay off, the joke
didn't land.
When he stormed off
downstairs,
he slammed the door
so hard it shook the walls.
I don't remember
whose birthday it was,
which makes me think
I don't want to remember
it was his.

WHEN THE PHONE RINGS

Andrea answers it, accepts the charges,
and we pass the phone around,
wishing my dad a happy Thanksgiving
at a distance, and I think

the hardest part about
how the phone calls work is that
if you're not in the mood to talk, if you're
sad, you're mad, you're happy,
you aced a test this week, or

you're racing out the door
to a life outside—
too bad, this is the time you get,
this is the call they waited in line to make.
And you're a bad person
if you want it another way.

Calling, calling.
This is someone you love.
Answer it. Answer them.

When it's my turn and my dad says,
Honeybee, I'm lonely today,
I feel my head get heavy. I say,
I'm sorry. Sometimes it feels like
all I can say.

My mom speaks sweetly into the phone—
We miss you too, she says, and I think,
who is *we* and do I know them?

FIRST NIGHT

My mom has the menorah out, along with purple-blue striped candles. Its slim gold branches, dotted with years of candle wax.

I'm always afraid she'll burn her fingers, but she never does. Andrea, Leslie, and I stand around the table, waiting for my mom to start. We say the blessing together, the words imprinted on my brain, even when I forget what they mean. My mom covers her eyes while she says it.

Baruch atah Adonai Eloheinu Melech ha-olam, asher kid'shanu b-mitzvotav, v-tzivanu l'hadlik ner shel Hanukkah.

An Adonai I've yet to forgive.

But I'm trying, I am, with my hands hiding my eyes.

To believe.   And if not to forgive, then to let go.

There's another blessing for the first night, but I never remember it. I listen to my mom say the words alone, a prayer with a rhythm I know just well enough to hum.

On the table:

a box of gelt, the wooden and plastic dreidels for spinning, and the ceramic and glass ones just for looking.

I send Noelle and Maya a picture of gelt, a few bags of it—for winning and losing in dreidel and then for eating. My mom searches for the dark chocolate ones and she usually finds them. They get soft to the touch as we play.

Gimel. Hey. Nun. Shin. My mom wins, but we still split the pot.

AND THEN IT'S TIME FOR GIFTS

It's tradition. I don't remember when we started doing this. Or maybe we always have.

Andrea, Leslie, and I wait in Leslie's room with the door cracked, listening for any sound.

"DON'T COME OUT UNTIL I SAY YOU CAN!" my mom yells.

I keep my eyes closed anyway, just to be sure.

I was surprised when my mom said
there'd be a present each night—
"But they're small," she said,
"they're *tiny*!"

I search everywhere. An embarrassingly long time. On my hands like a dog, then from up on the couch like a giraffe. All these angles and I still find nothing.

Andrea finds hers right away, shakes it a little, and, laughing, announces what it is. My mom says, *Andrea!* but laughs because Andrea's right about what's inside: a votive candle.

But she couldn't guess the scent. It's Life's a Breeze, which smells enough like the ocean if you close your eyes.

Leslie keeps searching and then finds hers hidden behind a huge framed class photo of Andrea. It's a paintbrush, I guess one from a set.

My mom's good at this. "Do you want any clues?" she asks after I struggle for a while. When I relent, she tells me where it's not.

Finally, I open a cabinet I'd already checked, see something tiny, shiny, and blue tucked behind a stack of board games.

I unwrap my gift on the couch, Peanut pushing her nose into the torn paper.

Mine can only be—

a single colored pencil.   Blue.

I look over at my mom, who's beaming.

That's when it hits me. "Oh my god . . . Is it a box of eight?"
I feel like I might cry, the good kind, watching my mom make
a miracle from something simple.

ON THE THIRD NIGHT

Chris comes over and we eat rotisserie chicken
and baked potatoes with Leslie and my mom.

He gives me a slim rectangle wrapped in green paper.
It's a first edition of Sylvia Plath poems
    with bare, beautiful trees on the front and back.
The gray cover is laminated like a library book,
smooth in my hands.

It's the first
    and the nicest
        real gift any boy has ever bought me.

I say ohmygod and thank you and I love it
    with my hand on my chest,
        as if to keep my heart inside.

Keep it safe, steady, mine.

I want to stay in this moment,   but the moment passes.

"That is the most amazing thing," my mom says.

Leslie shakes her head, like *Whoa*. "Well done, dude," she says.

He lights the candles when my mom offers.
I look between them,   their easy conversation,
and I see what my mom sees—
        a boy who tries,
who wore a button-down for Hanukkah at his girlfriend's house.

And also: the dark wave of his hair.
His eyes.
His sometimes eyeliner.

The forearms I think are totally perfect,
the hairs there, how the veins in his wrists move in ways
that cloud my thoughts.

But I have this feeling, like an itch—this not-yet-a-full-thought
I can't say out loud, especially not to Maya—
like I'm holding my breath.

Waiting for Chris to lose interest in me.
    And for me to seem unhappy. Too unhappy.
                To cry without cause.
To think too long
    or talk too much about something my dad said or wrote.

        And dip into the deep end of this feeling.

Spiraling out in my head, I feel bad
    watching him smile at something my mom says.

Like a bomb counting down in a movie, red wire cut
in my hand,

I still want him,   or I want to want him,
    but I don't want to need him like this, too much,

the way that I do—

MAYBE

the only person I can count on
to be in the deep end with me is me.

NOVEMBER 30TH

Today we're playing dodgeball in gym, which is
less of a game and more of a battle.
I spend the whole period trying to hide
behind anyone I can on my side of the red line.
On the opposite team, Maya throws the ball
near me, so it looks like I'm already under attack,
a small mercy. But then she's out
with a ball to the knee.
I become our best player's shadow, the only way
to protect myself, until he's out
with a whistle blow
and then there's nothing left for me to do
but stand like a starfish, open for attack,
take the hit, and sit down.

ACCEPTANCE

When the ball hits me, I don't feel
powerless, like I expect to.

It hurts, but the worst of it,
the waiting,

is already over.

BABY

A Hanukkah letter
  from my dad arrives
on the sixth night.
  He writes a memory:

when I was new,
  him holding me
to his chest, still
  warming to the world.

That was me,
  I was his baby.

I hold the letter to my chest.

I let myself cry
  fat, silent tears.

He's away
  in a place where
time stops—
  and I'm not.

I'm on the outside,
  trying to grow up
into whoever
  I'm going to be.

WHO I AM

In *The House of the Scorpion,*
Matt has to prove he's more than a clone—
not just to the people who want to destroy him,
but also to himself.

Matt has the power to choose.

And he does: to be different, to rule differently,
to love differently,
and begin again
at the end.

He shares genes with the ruler, but
genes aren't a map or a key. I try to remember
genes aren't all that make me
me.

DECEMBER 3RD

Maya comes over after dinner. We sink into the couch and watch TV. She tells me about the photography project she's planning for winter break—glamour shots in the park, a kind of winter wonderland starring us.

Chris calls and when I let it go to voicemail, Maya doesn't say anything. I don't either.

But a few minutes later, she turns the volume down on *Legally Blonde* and asks if I want to take a quiz and I say okay and she looks at me and says, "True or false: you're happy with your boyfriend." Without rolling my eyes or telling her to back off, I say, "Define 'happy.'" She looks like maybe she knows all that I can't begin to explain.

I sit up. It comes out in one scrambled thought: "What if I'm never happy again? In my life, I mean. I have to live with this weight around my neck for *years*." I slump over, elbows on my knees on the couch. "The world expects me to move on. But I can't."

"Not the world," she says, pausing, "not everyone. And you know, if they do, fuck them. Do what you need to do to get through."

What if that's screaming, I ask, what if it's breaking things. Even better, she says. She stands outside with me when Peanut has to go, the air cold, electric against my cheeks. Tonight, I feel wide awake.

STILL DECEMBER 3RD

My dad tells me about the cat he saw in the yard yesterday,
where it must have come from, all these questions
I have that don't seem important, even if I want the answers,
even if the answers exist.

What are they, I want to ask the universe,
how does this end, I want to add, and how much did you know,
I want to ask my dad, though the recorded message cuts in
again to tell us we're out of time—

and my mom says we'll all go see him again soon,
before Christmas, before it gets crazy.
Crazy, I think, a word that lies dormant inside my head like
a volcano, where no one else can see it erupt.

THERE ARE MOMENTS

with Chris where
it doesn't matter
that I can feel
the idea
of the end
of us
like a lump
in my throat,
like when we're
in his room
not talking
about anything
and his hands find
my collarbone,
my thighs,
the kissing
more urgent,
faster
than before,
like a buzzer
only I can hear.

DECEMBER 7TH

But Chris keeps his phone face down on his nightstand.
I don't mention the next trip to see my dad.
We circle each other like fighters on a mat,
unprepared to make the next move.
If I could stay in the warmth of right now,
keep my eyes trained
on his face,
if there was nothing outside of this
to want
or fear,
if.

STILL DECEMBER 7TH, BUT WHO CAN TELL

Sleepless, I remember the time
I was nine and an airbag deployed

and spilled its contents
in my lap. I was asleep.

I'd had the seat reclined
all the way back

and I woke to the burning smell,

my mom's arm gashed
in the driver's seat.

We fumbled out of the car

in the dark,
which was still blue

and undented
beside a crooked stop sign

and the thick yellow line.

The aftermath was worse
than the crash:

a fender bender
a few miles from home.

In every rerun of this memory,

I stand in the grass
and wait for a siren to sound

in the distance—

IN DRAWING AND PAINTING CLASS

My dad and I used to rip pens from their cords at the bank
and take them home.

I don't know why I'm thinking of the cords themselves,
the silver balls, like garland,

as I outline tree after tree for my landscape.
Or the fact that I've been a thief,

keeping the cords curled in a drawer with no use for them,
the pens dried out.

I can't make a weeping willow hold its shape,
keep trying for the severe sweeping motion

of the one outside our house.
Our old house.

But the clouds above I can do—tufts of white and gray,
striping the top of the page.

I finish the sky without a sun.
When I sign my name in the corner, I loop it large and full.

My teacher asks if I'm sure it's done, the question mark
heavy, pointed. Look at it again,

there's more I could do.
I could add a swing set, a skyscraper, something to look at

beyond the few trees,
the clouds, the wash-away blues and greens.

But I'm tired of expectations—tired of having to be more,
give more, keep pushing.

I leave it at the back of the room on a ledge
with supplies to dry.

It's done when I say it's done.
And if I don't call it done, it might never end.

I text Chris, a little hopeful, a little sad,
to see if maybe he can meet me after school.

ON THE SWINGS

at the playground
I take a deep breath
and say I don't think
this is working,

I don't think this
is how I'm supposed
to feel, how I want
to feel right now,

can't talk about
everything tearing through
my head, what keeps me
awake at night,

what makes me
a little crazy
and a little sad
and really angry

but also makes me   me.

BREAKUP?

It feels more like a sprain,
a limp I can't walk off.

When he says he feels
    the same way,

his voice is cold
and strange to my ears

and he leaves me
there, on the swings.

I feel like a kid.
I pump my legs and go

higher and higher,
until I feel my chest

hammering in time
with the chains

in my hands. I don't cry.
I have no tears today.

When I get home,

I tell Leslie what happened
and she says,

Shit, Jiord, I'm sorry.
You should be with someone

who gets it, you know?

I ASK MY MOM

what she knew about my dad's business, what role she played in it, if she's still thinking about getting divorced, when, and why she didn't get divorced before he went to prison—like the answers will also tell me if losing Chris is right or just inevitable.

If everyone eventually slips through the cracks or if some of them come back. And how to tell the difference.

We're sitting on the couch after dinner, after my dad has called and I've told my mom, *I'm not here.*

"These are good questions," she says diplomatically. She shrugs. "What's not normal can . . . become your normal." I consider this. "People can get used to just about anything. I guess that's what happened with us."

The moods, the money. The sound of my dad's feet on the stairs, coming up from his office, a coin toss. Sitting in my closet, wanting to escape. Years of waiting, waiting for what?

"The house *is* quiet now," I say.

She sighs. Not sad, just . . . calm, I think. "It *sure is*."

I don't need her to be sorry.
I don't need anyone to be sorry.

It's just time for things to change.

ACCEPTANCE, AGAIN

There are some things I'll never know, facts and memories, even faces,
that will only get grayer with time.

All these blank spaces, I'll have to fill in again and again.

But maybe in time,

there will be fewer of them.

DECEMBER 9TH

Good riddance—

Maya says it without saying it.
"We're going to have fun" is what she announces in my room,

                    turning Taking Back Sunday up loud—
a song about being lied to. Heartbreak. About it being over.

I guess it's over.
Before Chris, I never had a real start.

I worry that missing him means I should still be with him.

But then I remember his coldness at the playground,
how he left me there, how I wanted him
                                        to want a different ending.
He didn't ask about my weekend plans, so he doesn't know
they include going to visit my dad.
Hours in the car. The nervousness that makes my scalp itch,
makes my teeth hurt, an invasive ache like a pebble in a shoe.

I don't text Chris. I won't.

I use the silent treatment as a weapon   and a shield.

My throat burns the more I think about it
    and about

the good things we share and the times

when I've been sure he's the one,

even when I'm sure I'm almost sure

I'm actually the only one for me.

But Maya and I shout along to every song, draw on
thicker eyeliner, take selfies,

and I don't feel locked inside my head.

NOT ALONE

The next morning,
Leslie reads me a poem she wrote
that's going to be published in the lit magazine at school

and every line is musical and hungry
and beats against my sternum like
a handclap.

I can't feel what either of my sisters feel.
I can only imagine, look through a dirty window,
a film over everything we are.

But even with closed doors and boyfriends and years
and misunderstanding separating us from ourselves
and each other,

there's something about the idea of us as a unit.
Like maybe we were all born in the same universe
for a reason.

ENOUGH

I pack the clear bag of quarters, my phone, and a new lip balm—everything else in our suitcase in the trunk. My mom smooths a strand of hair, changing lanes. Andrea sits in the passenger seat. Leslie sits with me in the back. I press my hands against my lap like a fallen house of cards.

No text from Chris,

who feels like a fading strip of sunlight I can't chase.

I get a bunch of hearts from my friends and one of the last selfies Maya and I took. I squeeze my phone like a Taser, like keeping it close will protect me.

I can't keep up with my thoughts. I tap my thumb along with the radio, which is Billy Joel, who's singing about a place that waits for you.

The thought knocks inside me like a pendulum.

I think about texting Britt. I think about which gaps might be worth bridging.

It's never too late to change our minds—

is a thing I tell myself because I don't want to do this,

don't want to be in this car heading toward a gate,

barbed wire,

the sounds of boots on the ground.

The vending machines.
The smell of plastic burning.
My dad shape-shifting like a shadow before my eyes.

At a rest stop
I wonder who I'd be if I stayed out here,
never returned to the car
or the rest of my life.

Andrea offers me some of the pretzels she bought, a sip of her energy drink. I take a long swig from the can. Leslie and I share a to-go cup of hummus. My mom says, *We're making good time.*

I see my reflection in Andrea's sunglasses. I try and fail to find the sun, hidden in the clouds.

When they let my dad into the room, I watch his eyes search for us,
his face closed off, hard in a way I don't remember.

Over in the kids' corner, SpongeBob dances to music I can't hear. The TV is old, mounted at an angle, like a security camera.

I put the sack of quarters on my lap. Leslie volunteers to hold them instead. Her hand on mine in here feels like a tiny electric shock, like a sweater fresh from the dryer.

He tells us how good it is to see us, that he can't wait to get out of here,
just wants to get out of here.

But right now, he wants a burger, whatever's heaviest. A spicy double cheeseburger costs five dollars in quarters, which we have.

I follow the rules—

I take one plate, one packet of ketchup, one packet of mustard, hold both in my hands, and microwave the burger on the plate until the plastic wrapper threatens to pop.

My dad examines my face while it cools on the plastic teal table between us, an abandoned bag of Cheetos there. He says I look so much like him. *You do, like it or not.*

My mom rubs his hand.
She asks how things are.

Andrea says he looks really good, healthy.

He tells us that a guard who he says
planted something contraband in his locker
was diagnosed with cancer.

He laughs loud when he says it,
the sound jolting me upright.

My mom winces. I imagine my face looks like Leslie's—a mix of sympathy and horror. Andrea changes the subject.

I think about the nail polish on Maya's floor. About Peanut curled on the couch. I look at the ceiling, I look at my hands, I trace each fingernail. I take long breaths.

I try not to disappear.   I try to stay right here.

There's a woman visiting another prisoner a few chairs down.

Out of the corner of my eye, I watch her cup his hands
as if they were delicate,
as if they were free of judgment—mine
and anyone else's.

No matter what happens, I tell myself,

I get to go home. I get to leave.
So I open the forgotten bag of Cheetos and
breathe.

In the car after, I text Britt: *Do you want to maybe talk on the phone this weekend?* My chest is thudding hard, like I've just asked someone if they like me too and I'm waiting for a note to be passed back in class.

The kind of thing that would have made Britt laugh in sixth grade, if she knew.

Maybe it still could.

Then I read through my last text to Chris, asking him to meet me at the playground. All the empty space that followed, all the things we'll never say.

And how I'll learn to be okay.

BACK HOME

I listen to an old recording of my dad: he's playing the guitar and singing.

A cover. It's a love song.

He used to ask me if he could be famous, if he was that good.

I used to sit beside him at the piano
and hammer on the black keys.

I get his keyboard out of its case. Without the sound on, I perform—not a song, not really, just muscle memory. My version. My idea of what a song could be.

ACKNOWLEDGMENTS

This book wouldn't be possible, *I* wouldn't be possible, without a lot of other people.

I want to acknowledge the countless children and families affected by incarceration in the United States. There are too many stories and sentences far worse and more isolating than what I've experienced or detailed here. Time doesn't heal all wounds, but the distance of years helped me let go and lay down parts of my own story on the page. For me, escape was never the point—freedom was. I wish all that and more for any teen or adult who reads this book and finds even an inkling of themselves in its pages.

The biggest, most precious thank you to Ashley Lopez, my true-blue agent and dear, dear friend. You saw the potential in my writing and me before anyone else on this wild journey, and all because you were willing to take a chance on an unknown poet. I hope we deliver on a thousand more dreams.

This book wouldn't even exist without Joy Peskin, my incredible editor. Whether it's fate or luck or some combination of the two, I thank every star in the universe I got to make this thing with you. You knew what to do with this story before I did and you made me brave enough to tell it.

The people who bring books to life deserve the world.

Everyone at FSG BYR who helped make this book into the physical fact of itself—its cover, its commas, all of it—thank you so much: Ilana Worrell, Celeste Cass, Samantha Sacks, and Hope Hushon. Especially to Hannah Miller for being a consistent beacon of light in my inbox and Mallory Grigg for conjuring the most perfect cover design. Thank you to Alexus Blanding for being such a generous authenticity reader and to Elisa Rivlin for providing legal expertise and posing such thoughtful questions. To my impossibly wonderful blurbers: Sara Nović, Robin Ha, Mariama J. Lockington, Ariel Henley, and Jennifer Moffett—thank you for your time, support, and every kindness.

At the University of San Francisco, I was fortunate to take several classes with Ryan Van Meter, who opened my mind to the possibilities of experimental nonfiction as an undergrad. I wrote the first version of "The Visit" in his class more than a decade ago and it took me somewhere I couldn't go before. D. A. Powell, Father Sean Michaelson, Kimberly Garrett, Dean Rader, Susan Steinberg: in different ways, you all taught me. I was homesick and then suddenly I was home.

To Catherine Barnett, Donna Masini, and Tom Sleigh, my poetry professors at Hunter College: I joke that I spent two years working full time, getting my MFA full time, and crying full time, but the truth is that you gave me the gift of finding my way forward in poetry and back to myself. I left with a thesis that became a blank page that became this book. All of it mattered. Same goes for my talented and loving Malibu Crew: Jenna Breiter, Eric Janken, Vanessa Ogle, Mari Pack, Sam Reichman, and Jamie Smith. To Grace Schulman, my fairy godmother of poetry, thank you for allowing me to spend time with your memoir and to be a fly on the wall of your writing life for a semester.

Other people and organizations that have played a role in my arrival at this particular book: Paul Lisicky and every genius writer and friend I met at the Juniper Writing Institute; Blue Stoop and the students who became friends; Paragraph for the gift of time and space; Dr. Nechama Fertig, without whom I would be in worse mental and dental shape; Christopher Larkin for composing the music for *Hollow Knight* (much of this book was written to it); Cloud Cult and AFI for long years of rabid fandom; Derek DelGaudio and Justin Willman for all the hours of magic.

To a multiverse of creative friends who've been along for different versions of this ride, whether championing this book or supporting me or my dog or all of the above: Hannah Bae, Lauren Berry, Carl Braun, M.M. Carrigan, Colton Childs, David Emery, Michele Filgate, John Gorup, Lauren Hilger, Brad King, Michael Kleber-Diggs, Nicole Klemp, Samantha Lapierre, Michael Lepore, Sara Lippmann, Natasa Marinkovic, Matt Mastricova, Isle McElroy, Katherine D. Morgan, Bill Neumire, Tim O'Grady, John Rice, Chris Rose, Christina Rosso-Schneider, Rebecca Rubenstein, Danielle

Shoshani, Sharlena Shy, Eric Smith, Wes Solether, and Alisson Wood.

Nicole Steinberg, my rock, my unofficial lawyer: In my heart, it's always laundry day and we're always becoming the best of friends. Jessie Nicely, Cookie, my bone broth: Craigslist made us a family. Thanks to you and the incomparable Jaya Nicely for always letting me participate in *Compound Butter*. Let's eat.

Elizabeth Mazzarella, I could never write a better friend than you were to me when we were teenagers; I'll always remember our first sleepover at your house, how it felt to be known. Tara Baron, you're the pretty room and everything in it—don't ever forget that. Molly Burnett, my forever prom date and the brightest heart I know. I wouldn't have made it through middle school or high school (or this moment, right now) without all the love in this real-life group chat.

To the other friends who loved me or were even just *kind* to me growing up: thank you—I didn't forget and I never will. Two of the closest friends I had during the early events of this book are no longer with us; I wish they were.

To my family, the first one I knew: all of you, then and now. Lez, you're the petals in my pocket, a stunning reminder to come home. Mom, for believing in me even when all I did that one year was put sprinkles in my cereal and take the F train to sell cupcakes. Thank you for loving me, even though I wrote this book and put a brick through the past.

To Jerrod's family, who have all always accepted me as fact, as family without an asterisk. Bishop, Brown, Chaffee, Morgan, Paternostro, Rogers, and all variations of our last names and area codes: I won the lottery when I inherited you all. Get in the car, we're going to Graeter's.

To Hacksaw, the dog I was destined to meet. Our king baby. Everything I have is yours.

To Jerrod, my happy thought, my lucky charm. Thank you for listening to every single thought I have as I have it. For folding the laundry. For ordering dinner so I could lose myself in language. For being you, and in doing so, making me happier than I ever knew I could be.